THE ANFAL CAMPAIGN IN IRAQI KURDISTAN

THE DESTRUCTION OF KOREME

the Forced Relocation of its Inhabitants,
the Massacre and Disappearance of its Men and Boys,
the Chemical Weapons Attack on the Village of Birjinni,
and the Death of Farwan Tawa Mostafa, a Female
Infant, at Beharke Camp, in the course of the 1988 Anfal
Campaign against the Kurds of Iraqi Kurdistan by the
Government of Saddam Hussein

Oral Testimony and Physical Forensic Evidence

A Report by
Middle East Watch
A Division of Human Rights Watch

and

Physicians for Human Rights

Human Rights Watch
New York • Washington • Los Angeles • London

Middle East Watch
Middle East Watch was established in 1989 to establish and promote observance of internationally recognized human rights in the Middle East. The chair of Middle East Watch is Gary Sick and the vice chairs are Lisa Anderson and Bruce Rabb. Andrew Whitley is executive director; Eric Goldstein is research director; Virginia Sherry and Aziz Abu Hamad are associate directors; Suzanne Howard is associate.

Physicians for Human Rights
Physicians for Human Rights is an organization of physicians and other health professionals that brings the knowledge and skills of the medical sciences to the investigation and prevention of violations of international human rights and humanitarian law. Since its founding in 1986, it has conducted over forty missions concerning twenty-five countries.

Physicians for Human Rights works to apply the special skills of health professionals to stop torture, "disappearances" and political killings by governments and opposition groups; to report on conditions and protection of detainees in prisons and refugee camps; to investigate the physical and psychological consequences of violations of humanitarian law and medical ethics in internal and international conflicts; to defend the right of civilians and combatants to receive medical care during times of war; to protect health professionals who are victims of human rights abuses and to prevent physician complicity in torture and other human rights abuses.

Physicians for Human Rights adheres to a policy of strict impartiality and is concerned with the medical consequences of human rights abuses regardless of the ideology of the offending government or group. The President of the Board of Directors is H. Jack Geiger, M.D.; the Vice President is Carola Eisenberg, M.D. Eric Stover is executive director; Susannah Sirkin is deputy director and Barbara Ayotte is senior program associate.

To the townspeople of Erbil who, risking themselves, provided for the villagers of Koreme and thousands of others in the camps of Beharke, Jeznikam, Qushtapa, Daratu, Binasirawa, Kasnazan, Sharways, Pirzin, Mala Omar, Segirtkan, Barhushtar, and Sebiran when they were hungry, unsheltered and in great need.

Until [Lidice], there were supposedly only two possible attitudes for a conqueror toward a village that was considered rebellious. Either calculated repression and cold-blooded execution of hostages, or a savage and necessarily brief sack by enraged soldiers. Lidice was destroyed by both methods simultaneously ... Not only were all the houses burned to the ground, the hundred and seventy-four men of the village shot, the two hundred and three women deported, and the three hundred children transferred elsewhere to be educated in the religion of the Fuhrer, but special teams spent months at work leveling the terrain with dynamite, destroying the very stones, filling in the village pond, and finally diverting the course of the river. After that, Lidice was really nothing more than a mere possibility ... To make assurance doubly sure, the cemetery was emptied of its dead, who might have been a perpetual reminder that once something existed in this place.

Albert Camus,
The Rebel*

---

*Copyright 1956 by Alfred A. Knopf, Inc.; used by permission.

TABLE OF CONTENTS

APPENDICES

Acknowledgements

This report was written by Kenneth Anderson, director of the Arms Project of Human Rights Watch, and edited by Andrew Whitley, executive director of Middle East Watch, a division of Human Rights Watch; Aryeh Neier, executive director of Human Rights Watch; Kenneth Roth, deputy director of Human Rights Watch; and Eric Stover, executive director, Physicians for Human Rights. It was reviewed by Jemera Rone, counsel to Human Rights Watch, and Mostafa Khezry and Joost Hilterman, consultants to Middle East Watch.

This report is based on investigations carried out by a forensic team composed of distinguished international experts in forensic anthropology and archaeology organized by Middle East Watch and Physicians for Human Rights. The forensic team's mission to Iraqi Kurdistan took place between May 26 and June 22, 1992.

Members of the forensic team were:

° Kenneth Anderson, forensic team leader. Mr. Anderson, a New York lawyer, is director of the Arms Project of Human Rights Watch.

° Luis B. Fondebrider. Mr. Fondebrider is a founding member of the Argentine Forensic Anthropology Team (Equipo Argentino de Antropologia), which has conducted exhumations of the graves of the disappeared in Argentina and throughout Latin America. The Argentine Forensic Anthropology Team's forensic evidence was regarded as crucial in securing convictions of several members of the Argentine police and military. Mr. Fondebrider has also worked on forensic exhumations in Chile, El Salvador, Guatemala, and other places.

° James Briscoe, forensic team archaeologist. Mr. Briscoe is an archaeologist with Roberts/Schornik & Associates, Inc. of Oklahoma. He has extensive experience conducting archaeological digs in the Americas. The forensic team is grateful to Roberts/Schornik & Associates, Inc. for making Mr. Briscoe available for an extended period of time in Iraqi Kurdistan. It is also grateful to Roger Burkhalter for his assistance with computer graphics.

° Mercedes Doretti. Ms. Doretti is a founding member of the Argentine Forensic Anthropology Team. She has undertaken forensic exhumations in Argentina, Chile, Guatemala, the Philippines and, most recently, in El Salvador where she has been engaged in unearthing victims of the El Mozote massacre of December 11, 1981.

° Isabel M. Reveco. Ms. Reveco is a founding member of the Chilean Forensic Team (Grupo de Antropologia Forense de Chile). The Chilean Forensic Team has conducted forensic exhumations in cases resulting from the 1973 Pinochet coup against the government of Salvador Allende and subsequent repression by the security forces.

° Stefan Schmitt. Mr. Schmitt, a German national residing in Guatemala, is a founding member of the Guatemalan Forensic Team (Grupo

Antropologia Forense de Guatemala). The Guatemalan Forensic Team, with the assistance of forensic teams from elsewhere in Latin America, has recently begun work exhuming victims of Guatemala's security forces in the Guatemalan highlands.

◦ Clyde Collins Snow, forensic team scientific leader. Dr. Snow is a faculty member of the Department of Anthropology, University of Oklahoma, at Norman, Oklahoma. He is internationally famous for his work in Argentina and many other places worldwide. His work has been the subject of many articles, a book, and television documentaries. He has most recently been in Bosnia at the request of the U.S. Department of State to investigate allegations of war crimes there.

Photographs appearing in this report on pages [ ] were taken by Susan Meiselas and used by permission of Magnum, Inc.

Ballistics and firearms analysis was provided by Douglas D. Scott, Ph.D., of Lincoln, Nebraska, to whom MEW/PHR and the forensic team express their deep appreciation.

Maps were created by Michael S. Miller, a geographer in New York City who provides frequent assistance to Human Rights Watch.

The forensic team gratefully acknowledges the unflagging aid of Jemera Rone and Mostafa Khezry during its mission in Iraqi Kurdistan. It also thanks its local staff of translators and drivers who provided constant and often round-the-clock services on many occasions, as well as the many Kurds who provided testimony to the forensic team and the community of non-governmental organizations in Iraq that assisted the team with contacts and sources. The forensic team regrets that, for their protection, these persons cannot be identified.

Finally, the forensic team thanks Suzanne E. Howard, staff associate of Middle East Watch for her administrative help to the team before and during its work in Iraq. The forensic team thanks her and Barbara L. Baker, staff associate of the Arms Project of Human Rights Watch, for their work in preparing this report for publication.

INTRODUCTION

The report that follows does not record the full horrors of the 1988 Anfal campaign.[1] Such an account would describe the destruction of hundreds of Iraqi Kurdish villages and their inhabitants, which this report does not attempt.

Instead this is a case study of the disaster that befell a single Kurdish village, Koreme, and its population during the Anfal campaign. It aims to show, in the greatest detail, the nature of the crimes committed in 1988 by the government of President Saddam Hussein against one remote mountain village in northern Iraqi Kurdistan.

Middle East Watch (MEW), a division of Human Rights Watch, (HRW) and Physicians for Human Rights (PHR) believe the experience of Koreme is representative of what happened to thousands of Kurdish villages in the northern mountainous provinces of Iraq before and during the Anfal campaign. Subsequent MEW reports will document how the Anfal campaign was carried out across all of Iraqi Kurdistan. These reports will also analyze Iraqi government and army documents captured by Kurdish forces in the March 1991 Kurdish uprising in order to reveal the planning and intentions underlying Anfal.

The importance of Koreme's experience is not only the cruelty that occurred there but also that it was apparently characteristic of the practices against other villages -- large-scale murders, disappearances, forcible relocations, and destruction with the intent to destroy the village population of Kurds as such. If ongoing research confirms this pattern, the destruction of Koreme would emerge as a genocidal act, part of a genocide undertaken against the Kurds across all of Iraqi Kurdistan. Koreme would thus represent a genocide-in-miniature and would stand for the experience of thousands of other destroyed villages, the sufferings of whose inhabitants cannot be reported in such detail.

---

[1] "Al-Anfal" is the name of a Koranic Sura, "the eighth sura, The Spoils," a revelation to the Prophet Muhammad in the wake of the first great battle of the then-new Muslim faith at Badr (624 A.D.). See *The Koran*, transl. N.J. Dawood, Viking, 1990, at 176. The term "Anfal" refers to the plunder or spoils of the infidel, and was used by the Iraqi government to give a religious justification to its attack against the Kurds of Iraq, although they too are Muslim. This report refers interchangeably to the Anfal campaign or, for brevity, simply Anfal.

1

MEW/PHR do not suggest that the experience of Koreme, without more, proves genocide. Proof of genocide requires a showing of genocidal intent as well as a serious attempt to carry it out.[2] Crimes against a single village, no matter how vicious, cannot prove genocide. Nonetheless, research increasingly leads to the conclusion that the Iraqi government's Anfal campaign amounted to the crime of genocide within the meaning of the Genocide Convention. MEW/PHR will, as appropriate, formally make that case in future reports.

MEW/PHR are aware that genocide has been a much-used -- perhaps over-used -- word in recent months. Armed conflicts in the former Yugoslavia, the former Soviet Union, and other places have caused journalists, commentators, politicians, and diplomats to struggle for terminology with which to convey the terrors of ethnic conflict, ethnic cleansing, and violent ethnic chauvinism. Genocide is however a juridical term, with a legal definition established by treaty. It seeks to describe perhaps the greatest crime in the human canon. It is not a term ever to be used lightly or imprecisely. For that reason, we withhold definitive judgment on whether or not the Anfal campaign was genocide until our research is complete, although our research points steadily in the direction of a finding of genocide.

Although MEW/PHR withhold final judgment on the Anfal campaign as genocide, we have no hesitation in concluding that the events described in this report, constituting murder, forcible disappearance, involuntary relocation, the refusal to provide minimal conditions of life to detainees, chemical weapons attacks against civilians, and the physical destruction of Koreme, Birjinni, and other Kurdish villages are crimes against humanity within the meaning of customary international law. Crimes against humanity are a recognized international crime, for which defendants were tried and convicted at the Nuremberg Tribunal. The elements of crimes against humanity, set forth with greater specificity at Appendix 5 of this report, are murder, extermination, enslavement, deportation or other equally serious inhumane acts committed against any civilian population, or persecutions on political, racial, or religious grounds including equally serious

---

[2] See Convention on the Prevention and Punishment of the Crime of Genocide (the "Genocide Convention"), opened for signature Dec. 8, 1948, 78 U.N.T.S. 277 [1949], entered into force Jan. 12, 1951, reproduced as Appendix 4.

2

inhumane acts or crimes, whether or not in violation of the domestic law
of the country where perpetrated, and committed on a mass basis.[3]

Unlike genocide, crimes against humanity does not require proof
of intent, based on the racial, religious or ethnic identity of the victims,
to destroy a people as such, and it is thus easier to prove than genocide.
The events described in this report include murder, extermination,
deportation and such similarly inhumane acts as forcible disappearance
constituting murder. These acts took place in the context of racial
persecution of the Kurds in Iraqi Kurdistan, although it remains for
further research to determine conclusively that those persecutions were
intended to destroy the Kurds "in whole or in part...as such" within the
meaning of the Genocide Convention.

The determination that the crimes described in this report
constitute crimes against humanity is based in part on their mass scale.
MEW/PHR have obtained hundreds of eyewitness interviews in addition
to secondary press, and governmental accounts of such atrocities as
chemical bombardments of villages, the destruction of thousands of
Kurdish villages, and the murder, forcible disappearance, and involuntary
relocation of hundreds of thousands of Kurds during the Anfal campaign.
The evidence of these atrocities overwhelmingly fulfills the "mass scale"
requirement. Accordingly, MEW/PHR charge the government of Iraq,
the Ba'ath Party, and the Iraqi army with crimes against humanity and
we call upon the international community to undertake appropriate
measures to see that prosecution and punishment are carried out.

Although the purpose of this report is to trace in detail the plight
of one set of Anfal victims, the residents of the village of Koreme, the
events at Koreme are not just another sad story in the history of human
rights violations. What happened at Koreme are crimes, international as
well as domestic. In offering conclusions of fact and law, MEW/PHR
point out that the Iraqi government by the scope of its actions made itself

---

[3] See Appendix 5 for HRW's view of the legal elements of crimes against
humanity applied to the events described in this report. The elements named
above are drawn from the Charter of the International Military Tribunal, article
6 (c), as amended by the Berlin Protocol, 59 Stat. 1546, 1547 (1945), E.A.S. No.
472, 82 U.N.T.S. 284, as modified by the Judgment of the Nuremberg Tribunal,
International Military Tribunal, Judgment, 6 F.R.D. 69, reprinted in 41 *Am. J.
Int'l. L.* 172 (1947) and various Allied war crimes tribunals interpreting similar
language.

vulnerable to legal action by the international community. Our descriptions of the events at Koreme are formulated here as statements of crimes, and as a call to the international community to indict, prosecute and punish their authors.

Anfal's Pattern of Destruction Across Iraqi Kurdistan

The methods and patterns of destruction generally followed during the Anfal campaign across the northern region of Iraqi Kurdistan are summarized below; they were implemented in the microcosm of Koreme.

Anfal was a campaign of the Iraqi government and army carried out against the village Kurdish population of Iraqi Kurdistan in 1988, the year during which the Iran-Iraq War came to an end.[4] Anfal was a name used by the Iraqi army. Taken from a Koranic verse, it refers to "the plunder of the infidel," and evidently was intended to give the campaign the veneer of religious justification, though the Kurds themselves are Muslim and Iraq is a secular state.[5]

The Anfal campaign began in the southernmost Kurdish zones of Iraq. The Kurdish zones are located in northern Iraq; those bordering

---

[4] There is controversy as to where Anfal began and ended. Seen as an Iraqi military campaign, it began with the attack on the PUK guerrilla headquarters at Sergalou, near the Iranian border, on the night of February 25-26, 1988. It ended with the general amnesty of September 6, 1988, which marked the completion of what the Iraqi army referred to as the "Final Anfal" in the Badinan region. Alternatively, from the perspective of the victims, Anfal began with the destruction of villages and forcible disappearances following the fall of Sergalou in mid-March 1988; the campaign ended sometime in the fall of 1988. Despite the September 6 amnesty, some Yazidi Kurds, Assyrians, and Turkmen were disappeared after the military operation had ended. It was clearly, however, a campaign that began and ended in 1988. See generally Kanan Makiya, "The Anfal: Uncovering an Iraqi Campaign to Exterminate the Kurds," *Harper's Magazine*, May 1992; Raymond Bonner, "Always Remember," *The New Yorker*, September 28, 1992.

[5] See note 1.

Turkey and Iran are largely mountainous with villages in the valleys.[6] Over a period of months during 1988, the campaign moved northward. By late summer 1988, Anfal had reached the rural villages of the northernmost governorate of Dohuk, catching the inhabitants of those zones in a pincer movement between troops pushing northward and troops along the Turkish border pushing southward.

The broad pattern of destruction was similar throughout the campaign and the affected region, although there were variations from place to place, particularly between southern and northern Kurdistan; Koreme lies in northern Kurdistan. A village was often first shelled or bombed, sometimes with chemical weapons, evidently of the type used in the Iran-Iraq war. The inhabitants, attempting to flee, were trapped by troops enveloping the village. In two instances documented by MEW/PHR, Koreme and Mergatou (both in Dohuk Governorate) men and boys among the captured villagers were executed on the spot. Surviving villagers were then taken under guard, using a combination of regular Iraqi army troops, military police, and the reserve forces of the National Defense Battalions, to a local fort run by the Iraqi army or to a Ba'ath Party building, usually in the town nearest the village.[7]

At the fort, virtually all of the remaining men and older boys disappeared at the hands of security agents; the whereabouts of many tens of thousands of Kurdish males who disappeared in the hands of Iraqi government forces is unknown.[8] However, MEW has obtained reports from several eyewitness survivors of mass executions, who testified that the forcibly disappeared Kurds were taken south by truck and later killed

---

[6] For social and political overviews of the Kurdish people, see generally *People Without a Country*, ed. Gerard Chaliand, transl. from the French by Michael Pallis, Zed Press, 1980; Martin van Bruinessen, *Agha, Shaikh, and State: the Social and Political Structure of Kurdistan*, Zed Press, 1992.

[7] The National Defense Battalions also known colloquially as the "Jash"; this report will refer to it as the "National Defense Battalions."

[8] In the early part of Anfal, in the Germian region, men, women, children, and infants were also disappeared.

and buried in pits in various locations.[9] MEW/PHR believe that most, if not all, those who disappeared during Anfal were murdered by Iraqi security forces. Future MEW reports will detail the evidence for this opinion.

Surviving Kurds -- women, children, and the elderly -- were transferred by truck in a state of great hunger and privation, from forts to areas of southern Kurdistan. By the tens of thousands they were dumped in camps which lacked food, water, shelter or medical attention. These camps were simply empty land watched by guard towers. Many died there; those who survived did so with the help of essential supplies brought into the camps by Kurds in neighboring towns.

The Kurdish villages, empty of inhabitants, were then destroyed in their entirety under the direction of special teams of Iraqi army engineers. The rubble of thousands of Kurdish villages razed to the ground, down to the stone foundations of the schools and mosques, can be seen across Iraqi Kurdistan today. The mud brick houses were demolished with bulldozers and backhoes.

Anfal differed from earlier campaigns of destruction carried out by Iraqi authorities against the Kurds. The earlier campaigns had killed people and destroyed property, and were perhaps partly intended as punishment for presumed and actual collaboration between the rural civilian Kurdish population and Kurdish guerrillas, some of whom were aligned with Iran during the Iran-Iraq war. They were vicious and illegal campaigns, and constituted gross abuses of human rights. They were also apparently intended to reduce the Kurdish guerrillas' social base among the Kurdish villages and to relocate the Kurds, in part, into areas firmly under army control. But in contrast to Anfal, the earlier campaigns generally -- although not always -- assumed that Kurdistan was the Kurds' rightful place. Though the Kurds were liable to frightful punishment, they would remain where they had always been.[10]

---

[9] See MEW/PHR, *Unquiet Graves: The Search For the Disappeared in Iraqi Kurdistan, March 1992* ("Unquiet Graves").

[10] Not without exception, however; Kurds in large numbers were forcibly relocated during earlier periods, particularly from politically sensitive areas near the Iranian border and from other locations as well, and their villages were destroyed.

Anfal began from the different assumption that, foreseeing a possible ceasefire in the Iran-Iraq war, it was time to settle the "Kurdish problem" once and for all. It was not intended as exemplary punishment of the Kurds for their presumed or actual collaboration with Iran or for supporting Kurdish guerrillas. Punishment not being exemplary if there is no one left to witness the lesson, Anfal was not intended to deter. Anfal was a "final solution," implemented by the Iraqi government, the Ba'ath Party and the Iraqi army. It was intended to make the Kurds of Iraqi Kurdistan and their rural way of life disappear forever. Only such an intent can explain the precise, neat, and thorough destruction of the already empty Kurdish villages, and the fact that Anfal encompassed virtually all Kurdish villages. Or, as stated by Ali Hassan al-Majid, a cousin of President Saddam Hussein who was, during Anfal, in charge of Iraqi Kurdistan and at this writing serves as Iraqi Minister of Defense: "Yes, I'll certainly look after [the Kurds]. I'll do it by burying them with bulldozers. That's how I'll do it."[11]

The Investigation of the Anfal Campaign

Since mid 1991, when Kurdish fighters protected by the 1991 Gulf War allied forces established control over much of traditional Iraqi Kurdistan, permitting human rights monitors to enter the region, MEW has been conducting an investigation of the Anfal campaign. The investigation has had three parts.

First, MEW investigators have travelled throughout Iraqi Kurdistan, conducting interviews with survivors, in order to reconstruct the Anfal campaign, the extent of its destruction and the extent of its crimes.

Second, MEW, working with Kurdish groups in Iraqi Kurdistan, arranged to have large quantities of Iraqi government documents captured in the March 1991 Kurdish uprising airlifted to the United States in May 1992. MEW investigators have begun the task of

---

[11] Statement recorded on audio cassette tape, evidently during a speech to a closed-door meeting of regional security chiefs in the late 1980s. Along with large quantities of Iraqi army and government documents, it fell into Kurdish hands in the March 1991 Kurdish uprising. These materials are now being analyzed by MEW.

translating and sorting these documents in order to make available the evidence as to the Iraqi government's conduct of the Anfal campaign. The airlifted documents are some 14 tons, and the task of evaluating them is commensurately large.

Third, MEW and PHR assembled an international team of forensic scientists, under the scientific direction of forensic anthropologist Dr. Clyde Collins Snow (the "forensic team"), to undertake studies of mass gravesites reported to contain victims of the Anfal campaign.[12] The first MEW/PHR forensic mission took place in December 1991, and its investigations included a search for the graves of Anfal victims as well as of victims of Iraq's state security police and military during many years.[13] A second MEW/PHR forensic mission took place in February 1992, in which Dr. Snow and Andrew Whitley, Executive Director of Middle East Watch, tentatively assessed the mass gravesites discovered at Koreme, and made preparations to return for a full-scale exhumation in the spring of 1992.

The third MEW/PHR forensic mission to Iraqi Kurdistan took place between May 26 and June 22, 1992. Its mission was to exhume the gravesites at Koreme, take testimony, and conduct other investigations necessary for as complete as possible a determination of events at Koreme. Investigations were based on (i) forensic archaeology, to determine what structures had existed in Koreme and related sites, and the circumstances of their destruction, (ii) forensic anthropology, to identify victims and to determine the cause and manner of death of those found at Koreme and related sites, and (iii) oral testimony, taken from survivors, to construct a narrative of events at Koreme and related sites.

The forensic team was asked by MEW/PHR to gather evidence in as much detail as possible so to establish what happened at Koreme as if a case were to be heard before a judge, jury, or other trier of fact in accordance with internationally accepted standards of judicial due process.

---

[12] See Acknowledgments for the names and affiliations of the forensic team members.

[13] See *Unquiet Graves*.

MEW/PHR and the forensic team believe this effort has succeeded and that a court of law would accept both the account of events at Koreme and related sites presented below as well as the legal conclusions that follow.[14]

---

[14] This report contains no names of witnesses among the Iraqi Kurds, and indeed no full names of living Kurds. The risks to Iraqi Kurds posed by the Baghdad regime at the present time make this an unfortunate necessity. MEW/PHR are prepared to furnish this information to an appropriate body undertaking legal proceedings against the Iraqi government with appropriate guarantees of protection to the witnesses.

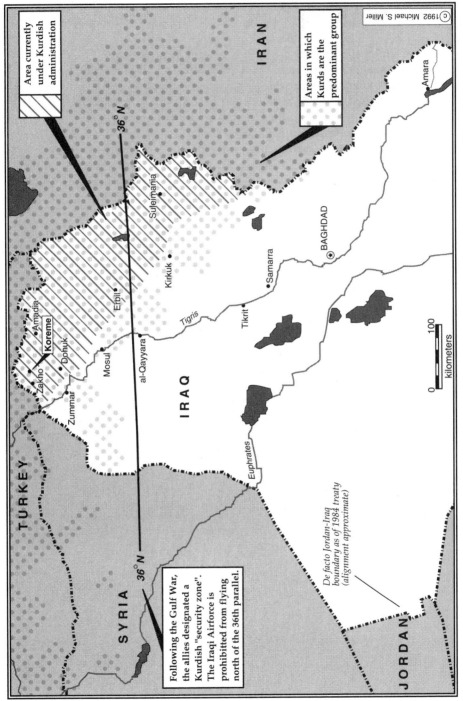

Area currently under Kurdish administration

Areas in which Kurds are the predominant group

© 1992 Michael S. Miller

Following the Gulf War, the allies designated a Kurdish "security zone". The Iraqi Airforce is prohibited from flying north of the 36th parallel.

De facto Jordan-Iraq boundary as of 1984 treaty (alignment approximate)

36° N

36° N

I R A N

T U R K E Y

S Y R I A

I R A Q

J O R D A N

Amara

Suleimania

Kirkuk

Erbil

Amadia

Koreme

Dohuk

Zakho

Zummar

Mosul

al-Qayyara

Tigris

Tikrit

Samarra

BAGHDAD

Euphrates

0   100
kilometers

Northern Iraq and the Kurdish Region

KOREME BEFORE THE ANFAL CAMPAIGN

The Anfal campaign was not the first time Koreme was attacked by Iraqi army forces. Koreme was partly or largely destroyed in periodic attacks that occurred during the previous two decades; the otherwise generally prosperous village had to be partly rebuilt at least three times between the early 1960s, when the Kurdish movement under Mostafa Barzani began in Iraqi Kurdistan, and 1988. Ironically, destruction occurred even during the greatest periods of Iraqi government investment in village infrastructure, such as electrification and building the village school. By the time of the Anfal campaign in August 1988, Koreme's inhabitants had largely abandoned the village site in favor of safer zones in ravines several kilometers away, near the hamlet of Hamsawa.

Despite partial destruction and the difficulties of living in hiding from army attacks, Koreme was still intact as a village prior to the Anfal campaign. Its inhabitants continued to work much of the village land. They retained their familial and tribal identities, and they remained Kurdish. The Anfal campaign, however, changed all of that. By killing or disappearing the village's men and teenage boys, forcibly relocating the surviving women, children and elderly to camps in the south, and razing the village to the foundations, the Anfal campaign sought to end Koreme as a physical and cultural entity, and it did so by the expedient of mass murder and disappearance. Anfal gradually has become a verb in the Kurdish language, and Koreme, like so many other Kurdish villages, was "anfalized." Following August 1988, Koreme was gone, and it is doubtful that it could ever have reestablished itself except as an unintended consequence of the 1991 Gulf War. It remains uncertain whether Koreme, missing so many men to perform agricultural work, will survive.

Pre-Anfal attacks on Koreme were repressive, brutal and destructive, but they accepted the premise that the village was there and would remain there.[1] The Anfal campaign, by contrast, started from the

---

[1] This was true of Koreme, but it was not true of many other villages. Numerous villages were destroyed and their inhabitants forcibly relocated in campaigns prior to Anfal; Anfal had precedents which it then carried to new, and qualitatively different, extremes. In the earlier campaigns, villagers were generally relocated to *mujam'mat*, or "collectives" -- large settlements near main

assumption that Koreme, and its Kurdish population, should not exist. For if Koreme did not exist, there would be no need to repress it.

---

roads and military bases where the population could be easily monitored. See MEW, *Human Rights in Iraq*, Yale U.P., 1990.

Plan of
Villages at
Koreme

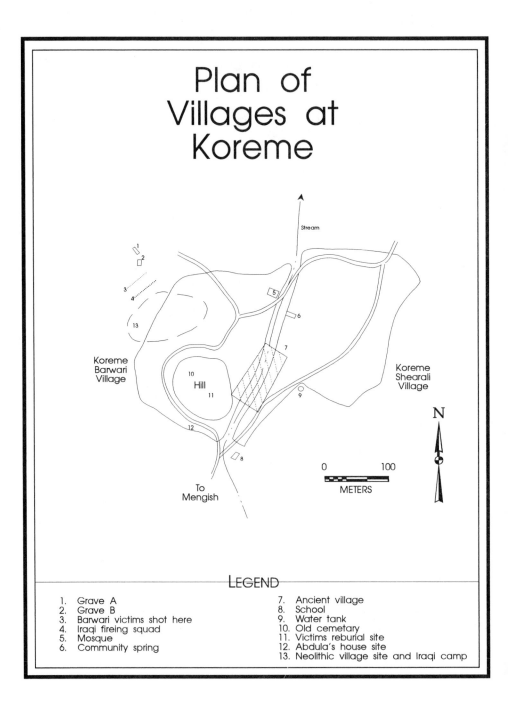

Stream

Koreme
Barwari
Village

Hill

Koreme
Shearali
Village

N

To
Mengish

0   100
METERS

LEGEND

1. Grave A
2. Grave B
3. Barwari victims shot here
4. Iraqi fireing squad
5. Mosque
6. Community spring

7. Ancient village
8. School
9. Water tank
10. Old cemetary
11. Victims reburial site
12. Abdula's house site
13. Neolithic village site and Iraqi camp

The Village of Koreme

Koreme is located in a small valley on the frontal range of the Zagros Mountains, about four kilometers north of the town and district capital of Mengish in Dohuk Governorate. Of ancient origin, it has an ethnically homogenous population of Kurdish Muslims. Koreme looks northward toward a mountain range about 50 kilometers away marking the border with Turkey.

Prior to 1988, the village population consisted of about 150 families, divided between the Barwari and Shearali tribes. Today, in 1992, survivors of the 1988 Anfal campaign and the March 1991 Kurdish uprising against the Baghdad government are slowly returning to the original village site, living in tents and lean-to's as they attempt to re-commence agriculture in their fields. Rebuilding is hampered by a scarcity of men and teenage boys who fell victim to the Anfal campaign, a lack of basic resources, and landmines.

Koreme prior to 1988 consisted of two clusters of buildings divided by a small stream running north-south through the center of the village (see Plan of Villages at Koreme). The principal landmark was a small hill some 10 meters high used as the village cemetery. There were originally about 100 to 150 houses in the village, including about 50 to 100 west of the stream belonging mostly to members of the Shearali tribe and about 50 east of the stream belonging mostly to members of the Barwari tribe. For some purposes, Koreme was regarded as two contiguous villages, divided by the stream and by clan affiliation; it appears on some government records of Dohuk Governorate as Upper Koreme and Lower Koreme. The village was governed by a group of village elders.

Houses in the village were not large, averaging approximately 5 x 8 meters, with a few larger structures interspersed throughout. Some houses were constructed of concrete bricks and limestone walls, often about 30 cm thick; most, however, were made of mud brick. There was also a village school and mosque; each building consisted of two rooms measuring approximately 15 x 20 meters, and constructed of limestone and reinforced concrete.

The school was built by the Iraqi government in the early 1980s and offered six years of classes. A teacher assigned by the government lived in the village until the school was partly destroyed by army attack in 1987 and classes were abandoned. Electricity was installed in 1987, shortly before army attacks that partly destroyed the village. Water came from local springs, but it was not piped to the houses and had to be carried by hand. Villagers received medical care from a clinic in the district capital of Mengish, about an hour and a half's walk. Motor vehicles could traverse the road, although only with difficulty in bad weather. The road from Mengish terminated at Koreme and there was no regular bus service, so most people traveled by foot or animal.

Agricultural lands border Koreme on the north, east, and west. The villagers raised a wide variety of cereals, grains and vegetables, including wheat and barley, peas, chickpeas, tomatoes, cucumbers, peppers, and onions. Orchards bore apples, pomegranates, and plums. There were also extensive vineyards. Villagers kept livestock, especially sheep, goats, cows, and chickens. Some of the fields were irrigated, while others relied on rainfall. The soil was good, and Koreme before the Anfal campaign was a prosperous village.

Koreme and the Peshmerga Guerrillas

Periodic attacks on Koreme over the years were motivated in part, according to local Kurdish guerrilla leaders today exercising political control in Kurdistan, by the Iraqi government's presumption that, taken as a whole, residents of traditional Iraqi Kurdish villages sympathized with Kurdish guerrilla organizations seeking autonomy from Baghdad. Koreme was one of many villages that suffered as a result of this presumption and does not appear to have been singled out for attack.

The Iraqi government's assessment of political attitudes among Koreme's villagers, according to surviving villagers, was broadly correct. According to survivors, Koreme villagers generally supported the guerrilla organizations that had ties to their particular tribe, which in the case of Koreme were guerrillas aligned with the Kurdistan Democratic Party (KDP). Over the years villagers had provided food, resources, and manpower to the KDP guerrillas who predominated in the region.

The Kurds call their guerrilla fighters "peshmerga," meaning literally "those who face death," and numerous Koreme men served or had served with the peshmerga, sometimes several generations of men in a single family. Typically, active peshmerga in this region at the time of the Anfal campaign served fifteen days on-duty with their unit, and fifteen days at home tending to fields.

It was not possible to establish from interviews how many of the Koreme men were active peshmerga at the time of the Anfal campaign; some were active fighters and others simply provided food or other assistance or were merely sympathetic. In 1992, with guerrilla organizations currently in control of parts of Iraqi Kurdistan, people generally prefer to identify themselves as peshmerga. Nonetheless, interviews established that some, perhaps many, Koreme men had served or were serving with the peshmerga either at the time of the Anfal campaign or during the immediately preceding years. For many, it was simply a way of life.

Peshmerga units passed through Koreme with some regularity, according to villagers, and at times provided rudimentary social services. For example, in 1987 villagers reported being afraid to seek medical services at the clinic in Mengish because the army had set up roadblocks on the road to Mengish and were arresting people, particularly men and boys. Indeed, several villagers reported that the government prohibited them from using the Mengish clinic, apparently because the village was considered disloyal, and that at least one man died from lack of medical care. A peshmerga doctor circulated among the villages during that period, carrying medicines on his back.

Battles between peshmerga and government forces were rare in the area immediately around Koreme, villagers said, and tended to take place in strategically more significant locations. However, for control purposes in the early 1980s, the government established a small military outpost on a hill between Mengish and Koreme. It overlooked the village and served as an artillery emplacement during various punitive bursts of shelling.

Although Koreme villagers provided material support to the peshmerga, they said that the peshmerga never had an established military base in the village or other facility that would qualify as a legitimate target in war. The nearest of the (frequently shifting) peshmerga military posts, at the time of the Anfal campaign, was reportedly half a day's walk or more away.

Koreme, unlike some other villages in the region, did not have a unit of the "Home Reserve Guard" or "National Defense Battalions." Known colloquially as the "Jash," the National Defense Battalions was a reserve unit of the army which utilized local Kurdish men, based in a local town or village, and used as a backup force in counterinsurgency operations against the peshmerga. Some recruits were persuaded to join by money payments and others were forcibly drafted. Still others joined on the basis of tribal and clan affiliations, either individually or together with the other men of their village or town. A village without the

National Defense Battalions was reportedly often regarded as suspect by the government.[2]

Attacks on Koreme Prior to the Anfal Campaign

Villagers generally identified three major occasions prior to the Anfal campaign, among numerous army attacks over the years, when Koreme was largely destroyed. The first, in 1963, followed an uprising against the government by Kurdish villagers; Koreme, older villagers reported, was virtually burned to the ground.[3] Its inhabitants fled into the mountains, and returned only several months later following the announcement of a government amnesty.

The second occurred in the late 1960s (with some disagreement among the villagers as to the exact year); on this occasion the village was extensively shelled and, after the population fled into the mountains, the army entered the village and destroyed more houses. It took the villagers about three years to rebuild following this attack. Many other villages in the area were also largely destroyed at this time, and for several months the people lived away from the village, hiding in caves found in ravines that crisscross the region.

The third occasion was in 1987. Fighting intensified between the government and the peshmerga in the course of the Iran-Iraq war, as some guerrilla groups materially supported the Iranians against Baghdad. Koreme suffered increasing numbers of artillery attacks and air bombardments during 1986 and 1987, over a year earlier than the notorious chemical gas attack on the Kurdish town of Halabja in March 1988 by the Iraqi army and air force, in which thousands of civilians died. Many village buildings were partially or wholly damaged, including the village school, which had been built by the government on a few years earlier. Classes ceased, and the government-assigned teacher returned

---

[2] During the Anfal campaign, however, even having a National Defense Battalions contingent was no guarantee of immunity from attack; various villages with Popular Militia were destroyed in the same manner as other Kurdish villages.

[3] For a general account of the beginnings of armed conflict between Kurdish guerrillas and the Baghdad government in the early 1960s, see Schmidt, *Journey Among Brave Men*, Atlantic Monthly Press, 1964.

to live in the city of Dohuk.   During 1987, the villagers gradually moved out of Koreme and into the ravines a kilometer or two down-valley. In the banks of the ravines were caves -- ledges, in fact -- cut by water drainage. The overhanging ledges were walled up in front to provide shelter. These caves had been used for generations to hide from hostile government forces. They were wet, cramped and dangerous. Formed of sand and earth, with large embedded stones, the roof of a ledge would occasionally collapse, sometimes crushing anyone beneath. Created by water seepage, the caves were damp and muddy, particularly in winter when several feet of snow fell. They did, however, provide shelter from shelling, bombardment, and capture by Iraqi army patrols.

The villagers went out by night to farm the fields nearest the ravines and furthest away from the army outpost overlooking the village. Sometimes they were shot at and pursued by soldiers, and sometimes their plantings were destroyed. It was never clear to them why army pressure was relaxed during some months, allowing them to farm relatively freely, while at other times it was implacable, with infantry sweeps and bombardments making it impossible to leave the caves for days at a time.

The Koreme villagers were joined in the caves by former residents of Chalkey, a village several hours away by foot. Chalkey had been destroyed by the army years before, and the residents had been prohibited from returning to rebuild it. Since the villagers of Koreme were closely related to those of Chalkey, they joined them in the ravines.[4]

The villagers continued to live in the caves during the early months of 1988, unsure when they might return home. On August 8, 1988, meanwhile, Iran and Iraq agreed to a ceasefire, freeing Iraqi army

---

[4] Chalkey has a long and sad history of its own. According to surviving villagers, it was largely destroyed in army attacks in 1976-77, and its inhabitants were forcibly relocated to the "collective camp" of Hisawa, near the city of Zakho. They remained there, under close government control, for about five years and were forbidden to return to their own village. When the Iran-Iraq war began, many of their sons, some of them peshmerga sympathizers, evaded the draft. In 1982-83 the families fled Hisawa in 1982-83 with their sons, to the village of Hamsawa, very near the ravines of Koreme. They remained in Hamsawa until shortly before Anfal when, because of increasing attacks, they joined the Koreme villagers in their caves. Thereafter the two groups traveled together, in an attempt to reach Turkey in August 1988, described in the next chapter.

units for operations elsewhere. High on the list of those operations --
something long in the planning, to judge by Iraqi army documents later
captured by Kurdish forces -- was a campaign to settle the Baghdad
regime's Kurdish problem, the campaign called "the plunder of the
infidel," or, the Anfal campaign.

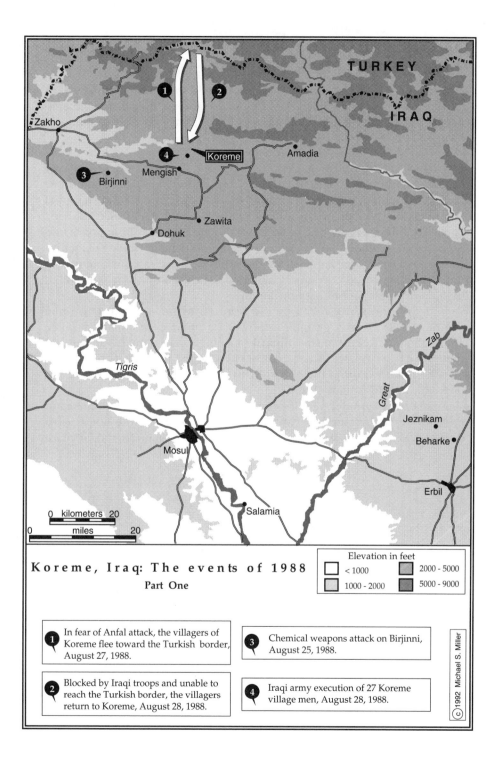

Koreme, Iraq: The events of 1988

Part One

Elevation in feet

- < 1000
- 1000 - 2000
- 2000 - 5000
- 5000 - 9000

1 In fear of Anfal attack, the villagers of Koreme flee toward the Turkish border, August 27, 1988.

3 Chemical weapons attack on Birjinni, August 25, 1988.

2 Blocked by Iraqi troops and unable to reach the Turkish border, the villagers return to Koreme, August 28, 1988.

4 Iraqi army execution of 27 Koreme village men, August 28, 1988.

© 1992 Michael S. Miller

FLIGHT TO TURKEY

Iraqi army attacks on Koreme prior to the Anfal campaign, as described by surviving villagers, were indiscriminate, illegal, and violated norms of both international human rights and international humanitarian law.

The fact that some, most, or even all of Koreme's inhabitants may have sympathized or materially supported the peshmerga can never excuse abuses of human rights committed in the name of counterinsurgency. Governments have wide powers under international law to deal with persons who materially aid internal insurrection or participate in insurgency in violation of domestic law.[1] Those powers do not however include shelling, bombing, and destroying whole villages on the basis of presumed support for the rebels; collective punishments; or indiscriminate attacks on noncombatants. Such measures are forbidden by human rights and humanitarian law.

Still, measures taken by the Iraqi government against Koreme prior to 1988 were recognizable as repression against a population which, although subjected to extraordinarily brutal, indiscriminate, and illegal methods of control, was still tacitly acknowledged to be in its place, viz., its traditional Kurdish lands. It was, strictly speaking, repression of the population, rather than elimination of it.

By the summer of 1988, the villagers of Koreme-in-hiding began to hear of attacks on Kurdish villages and towns to the south of a different caliber and strategic aim than anything that had taken place

---

[1] International law recognizes the power of states to maintain order within their borders, including suppressing rebellion, insurrection, and insurgency. However, there are two categories of restriction on their powers: (i) non-derogable human rights, such as those made non-derogable under Article 4 of the International Covenant on Civil and Political Rights, and (ii) international humanitarian law applicable to non-international armed conflict, such as common Article 3 of the Geneva Conventions. Neither body of international law prohibits rebels from being "punished under municipal law and there is no obligation to treat them as prisoners of war." Heather A. Wilson, *International Law and the Use of Force by National Liberation Movements*, Oxford University Press, 1988, at 23.

before. They did not know then the name of the operation, nor did they know its full extent or ambitions.[2]

The villagers did know, however, that a wave of violence was sweeping northwards. It included destruction on an unprecedented scale and attacks with chemical weapons. Part of this they learned from displaced people fleeing northwards; the peshmerga had also begun in 1987, following gas attacks, to provide instruction on crude protection against chemical weapons, usually consisting of breathing through a wet cloth or lighting fires. The villagers of Koreme were not easily frightened; they had endured destruction and the shocks of a largely one-sided war several years. Yet what they had heard by late August 1988 was enough to persuade them to undertake the difficult and risky flight on foot to Turkey -- itself a highly uncertain haven for the Kurds.[3]

Anguished Decisions

During the weeks before August 27, 1988, Koreme villagers saw many signs that the Anfal campaign was about to break upon them.

A woman took her daughter to a local healer in a small town to treat a sore on her hand and saw many troops and vehicles. Her husband, later executed at Koreme, told her the army was merely

---

[2] Although Koreme villagers did not know the full extent of the Anfal campaign, the extraordinary violence of the campaign -- especially the use of chemical weapons -- and the volume of refugees it caused to flee into Turkey and Iran brought some media attention in the West. See e.g. *Int'l. Herald Tribune*, "Messages Said to Indicate Use [of Chemical Gas Against Kurds]," Sept. 16, 1988; *Financial Times*, "Kurds Flee Iraqi Army Into Turkey," Sept. 5, 1988; *Le Monde*, "Des centaines de civils Kurdes ont ete tues a l'arme chimique par les forces irakiennes," Sept. 5, 1988; *Tribune Juive*, "Iraq Plans to Relocate Kurds from Mountain Habitat," Sept. 20, 1988; *Int'l. Herald Tribune*, "UN Is Asked to Check Reports on Kurds," Sept. 14, 1988; *The Washington Times*, "U.S. Protests Iraqi Use of Chemical Weapons on Kurds," Sept. 9, 1988; *The Independent*, "Iraqi Deal Threats Halt Kurd's Escape," Sept. 6, 1988; *The Sunday Times*, "Kurds Flee Chemical Terror into Turkey," Sept. 11, 1988; the *N.Y. Times*, U.S. Asserts Iraq Used Poison Gas Against the Kurds," Sept. 9, 1988.

[3] See *Int'l. Herald Tribune*, "Taking In the Fleeing Kurds: Turkey Treads a Difficult Path," Sept. 9, 1988; *Sydney Morning Herald*, "Ankara Shuts Door on Kurds Fleeing Iraq," Sept. 1, 1988.

replacing National Defense Battalions units with regular troops. Their 18-year-old son Nausad, who later disappeared at Dohuk fort and who had made regular trips to Turkey to buy food, also reported seeing many Iraqi soldiers and Kurdish refugees at the border.

Nausad believed, his mother said, that "something serious was underway." He thought the family should go to Turkey while there was still time; they could use his connections to get across the border. But his father believed it would be better to stay. The peshmerga, he said, would fight a holding action against the government soldiers, providing a screen behind which the families could escape. Besides, his father said, he had money and could bribe the army even if the family was captured.

Many families had such discussions in the days immediately before August 27. Some families fled earlier and made it over the border. Some decided to stay. Others decided to flee further into the mountains of Iraqi Kurdistan; one father told the other village men that it was better to "be hungry in the mountains of Iraq than to be shot by Turkish troops at the border" trying to keep them out. Another man decided not to take his family and flee because he thought the mines laid at the border by both Iraqi and the Turkish forces made the trip too dangerous. Still another man prudently left early for the border with his family; he later discovered, from a refugee camp in Turkey, that his brother's family, which had stayed behind, had all perished.

By August 23 and 24, aerial bombardment around Koreme had begun, shelling was nearly nonstop, and villagers saw helicopters dropping troops into nearby areas. No chemical weapons were reported at Koreme, although they were used extensively in the areas around it.[4] So on August 25 and 26, the main body of Koreme families, together with their relatives from Chalkey, decided, as one villager recalled, "that for us, time had run out and we had to try and reach Turkey."

Estimates by survivors of the number of Koreme people who fled range between 40 and 70 families, or 200 to 350 individuals. The best guess is perhaps 250 people, together with as much of their livestock as they could shepherd along. This number included perhaps 60 men and teenage boys who were later targets of execution and disappearance. The

---

[4] See Staff of Senate Comm. on Foreign Relations, 100th Cong., 28 Sess., *Chemical Weapons Use in Kurdistan: Iraq's Final Offensive* (P. Galbraith & C. Van Hollen, Jr. auth. 1988) ("Galbraith & Van Hollen") for lists of villages attacked with chemical weapons in Dohuk governorate.

number of adult and teenage males was lower than might have been expected, for several reasons. First, some men were fighting with the peshmerga and were not with their families. Second, some men correctly realized that they were likely to be singled out by the army, so they refrained from fleeing with their families toward the Turkish border, or took other evasive steps.

Flight

The Koreme villagers gathered together "what they could carry," survivors said, including food for several days. They put the elderly and infirm "on the horses that were left," and set off on the morning of August 27. Some started out a day or so earlier while others waited until evening to be less conspicuous. To evade army patrols, they avoided main roads and tried to avoid even minor roads, traveling more or less cross-country. The route made progress slow. In addition, the whole countryside was filled with thousands of others attempting to flee. Planes flew overhead, and on occasion they "were forced to hide in the brush" to avoid harassing gunfire.

The main body of families went first to Hamsawa, near the ravines, where some of the Chalkey families joined them. The group then continued to the village of Deje.

On the road they met people who told them of chemical attacks taking place that very day, August 27, in villages nearby. Koreme villagers described the people they met as "terrified and disoriented." These were people who had survived shelling and aerial bombardment for years, but chemical gas attacks from the air created unprecedented terror.

Concerned that they, too, might be attacked with chemicals in the open countryside, Koreme's village elders and family heads decided to send several younger men ahead to investigate conditions. One of those sent was Nausad, driving a flock of goats. He arrived in the village of Warmeli sometime soon after it was bombed with chemical weapons on August 27.

The Village of Warmeli

Nausad told his parents when they arrived later with the main body of families that he had seen planes flying around Warmeli as he came toward it on the road with his goats. There was smoke in the air, and he did not know whether or not it was poisonous chemicals or when the attack had taken place. But he saw people fleeing the village in terror, screaming and weeping. He hid in the brush above the road and did not approach any closer to the village at that time. His eyes were affected as the smoke drifted toward him, and he felt nauseated. As he later told his mother, his cousin had gone ahead toward the village and was "burned" on the exposed parts of his body, although he survived. Some of the animals died on the road; Nausad told his mother they just "fell over and after a little while stopped breathing."

Inhabitants of Warmeli who survived the chemical attack said that it occurred about 6:00 a.m. on August 27. Seven planes flew circles around the village, according to Warmeli villagers, and then two planes each dropped one bomb containing some kind of chemical smoke. Other planes dropped bombs that caused fires. One old man said he saw a chemical bomb explode, releasing a "white and then yellowish cloud that rose and drifted" down into the valley. He reported that he and his family tried to escape the gas by running up the valley, but one of his adult sons was "trapped in the gas and breathed it many times." The son fell to the ground and remained there as the rest fled "and no one could help him because we didn't dare go back while the cloud was there."

After the smoke dispersed and the planes departed, the Warmeli villagers returned to their homes. The injured man was taken and washed with water many times. He was suffering from "suffocation, he couldn't breathe, and then he had vomiting and diarrhea. He couldn't concentrate on anything and he was disoriented." The family put him on a wooden board and laid him on the flat roof of the house. They and the rest of the Warmeli villagers decided to flee immediately to Turkey, according to Warmeli villagers, that same day, on August 27. Warmeli survivors reported four deaths and an unknown number of injuries from the chemical weapons attack.[5]

---

[5] The Warmeli villagers subsequently split into two groups: the families who reached safety in Turkey, and the families who returned to Warmeli and were captured by the army. The group that turned back did so because, according to witnesses, it was attacked by planes with machine gun fire and driven back down the road. They returned to Warmeli and were captured by soldiers who arrived two days later. Their history from that point on is similar to that of the Koreme residents. Taken to forts in Mengish and Dohuk, 39 of the village men disappeared and have been not seen since. The remainder of the population was

Meanwhile Nausad rejoined the main group of Koreme villagers, meeting them as they came up the road to Warmeli several hours later. By that time the Warmeli villagers were already hurrying out of the village toward Turkey. "Great fear" came on the Koreme villagers as they passed through Warmeli, only a few hours after the attack, and they "rushed through the village," not stopping to bury the dead, apparently the victims of gas, lying by the side of the road. "We left them there," said one Koreme woman. "We were scared to touch them, even though they looked like they were asleep." Another old man said, "we thought the planes would come back for us. We had to hurry away."

Return to Koreme

The Koreme villagers knew that a massive military operation was underway throughout the entire Dohuk region, from the news they gathered from displaced persons fleeing through the countryside. They knew it was a coordinated land and air attack of great ferocity. They knew chemical weapons were being used and were sowing terror. They knew the operation was directed against the villages and not strictly against peshmerga.

What they could not know, without access to Iraqi military plans for the operation, was that it constituted a massive strategic envelopment of the Kurdish rural population in the regions of Zakho, Dohuk and Zawita. Documents captured by Kurdish forces from the Iraqi army in the March 1991 Kurdish uprising clarify the scope of the operation. One document, "Analysis: The Operation of the End of Anfal" ("The End of Anfal"), apparently written by staff of the Command of the Fifth Corps of the Iraqi Army, sets out in minute detail certain aspects of the Fifth Corps' attack plans in the August 28 operation.[6] It states that the "pivot

---

eventually sent south to the camp of Beharke, where, according to villagers, another 60 or 70 women, children and elderly died.

[6] While "The End of Anfal" sets out in great detail tactical aspects of the Fifth Corps' role in the August 28 operation, it does not describe the role of other units also involved in the operation, such as the First Corps. It likewise describes only briefly the operation in relation to the months-long Anfal campaign. Koreme, in fact, does not appear in the document, although Mengish does, most likely because Koreme fell in the jurisdiction of other corps. Still, it is a highly

principles" of the operation were "to operate from the outside toward the inside so as to encircle the saboteurs and destroy them ... [and] to suppress the saboteurs and deny them any chance to flee."[7] Later it describes the aim of "aerial capabilities" as "obstruction of [the saboteurs'] withdrawal lines toward the Turkish borders."[8]

Operating from the "outside toward the inside" meant attacking from the south while simultaneously cutting off access to the Turkish border on the north, and squeezing the population in between. The Koreme villagers came to understand this at the end of the day on August 27, as they saw increasing signs that they were going to be cut off by the Iraqi army before they could reach Turkey. They came under increasing aerial attack, and had to hide under covering brush and trees. They gradually abandoned many of their animals along the roadsides and in the valleys, to make themselves less conspicuous targets and to permit them to move faster. Loss of the animals meant, however, less protection from landmines, for the animals could be used as an advance guard to detonate mines.

The Koreme villagers met more and more people on the trails returning unsuccessfully from trying to cross the border.[9] Near the village of Girke, they met people from villages near Mengish, who told them the border was closed and that the army would capture them if they went further. By the evening of August 27, the families of Koreme were

---

significant document for understanding the grand envelopment envisioned by the Iraqi army command.

[7] "The End of Anfal" at 2.

[8] "The End of Anfal" at 38. The document consistently refers to "saboteurs," implying armed combatant peshmerga. This is disingenuous. "The End of Anfal" discusses, at 33, the "magnitude of the engineering work needed for the destruction and removal of the remnants of the saboteurs and their premises ...." Since the "remnants" and "premises" of the saboteurs included every sign of Kurdish habitation in scores of villages, including Koreme, it is evident that "saboteur" meant simply any Kurd in the zone of operations. See Chapter VIII, The Destruction of Koreme.

[9] See e.g., *The Australian*, "Turkey Flooded by Refugees, Sept. 5, 1988; *Int'l. Herald Tribune*, "Turkey Says Iraqis Have Blocked Routes Used by Kurdish Refugees," Sept. 9, 1988.

asking themselves whether it would be better to return home. They had also heard rumors that an amnesty was supposed to take effect that would allow them to go home peacefully.[10]

And so, later that evening they returned to Koreme, with the animals they had kept through the day. It was a dangerous and difficult night. They feared capture by army patrols, whose locations they did not know. Artillery continued sporadically throughout the night. They went slowly; they worried that surrender to the army was not a wise thing to do. On the morning of August 28, they were still walking and only reached the outskirts of Koreme in the afternoon. The late August heat was oppressive and they stopped for water wherever they found it.

At the first sight of soldiers, just outside the village, the men and boys put their hands in the air to signal their surrender. They feared the soldiers would open fire as soon as they saw them and not let them surrender, but nothing happened. The army, accompanied by National Defense Battalions units, took them into custody. The militiamen herded away their remaining animals. The villagers were hungry, thirsty, exhausted, and frightened. They were uncertain what would happen next.

---

[10] In fact, the amnesty was not issued until a week later, on September 6. See e.g. *The Sunday Times*, "Kurds Flee Chemical Terror Into Turkey," Sept. 11, 1988 ("...the Iraqi president's offer of amnesty, announced last week").

The Chemical Weapons Attack on Birjinni

Fear of chemical weapons attack was a prime reason why the villagers of Koreme tried to flee to Turkey. It was also a prime reason why they decided to return to Koreme and surrender. They had seen close-up the effects of chemical bombardment in the village of Warmeli. They had seen the terror of the Warmeli villagers. They had seen the dead lying by the roadside, unburied. Thus, although Koreme and its families were never attacked chemically, a complete case history of Koreme requires understanding how chemical weapons attacks on villages were carried out during Anfal. For this reason, this chapter now leaves aside the narrative of Koreme's villagers and turns to the account of a chemical weapons attack on a village in the same region as Koreme.

The Decision to Exhume at Birjinni

The logical place to make an investigation of a chemical weapons attack would have been the village of Warmeli, since it was the place, located some three hours' walk from Koreme in the direction of Turkey, where the Koreme villagers arrived in the immediate aftermath of a chemical attack. For scientific and forensic reasons, however, Warmeli was not ideal. Although extensive interviews were carried out by MEW/PHR investigators with some families who had survived the attack and returned to Warmeli following the March 1991 Kurdish uprising, the relatives of those who had died in the chemical attack on August 27, 1988 could not be interviewed. They had managed to enter Turkey in 1988, remained there in refugee camps for over three years, and then dispersed to different locations after mid-1991, when conditions in Kurdistan made it possible for them to return.

As a consequence, direct eyewitnesses of the Warmeli chemical attack were not available for interview. Moreover, the victims had apparently remained unburied during several years, according to Warmeli villagers. They took MEW/PHR investigators to places where they said the bodies had been left, indicating that the skeletons were still there when they returned in 1991, and said that slides of earth following storms had partially covered them. They had heaped on more earth to complete the burial.

The MEW/PHR forensic team had hoped to find graves of persons who had been buried shortly after a chemical attack and in the same clothing they were wearing at the moment of the attack in order to determine whether residues or other evidence of chemical agents remained after so many years. It was not very likely that residues of an air-disseminated chemical agent would remain after four years, even on a body that had been immediately buried; it would be extremely unlikely in the case of an unburied skeleton exposed to the elements over several years.[1] Nonetheless, it was important for MEW/PHR to pursue the possibility as a scientific experiment; while lack of physical evidence would indicate little, the presence of chemical agents after exposure over four years would be an important forensic and scientific finding. But this experiment could not be carried out in Warmeli. Furthermore, without relatives and eyewitnesses to interview in Warmeli, positive identification of skeletal remains of persons who had died in the chemical attack would have been impossible.

For these reasons, the MEW/PHR forensic team did not exhume at Warmeli, and instead undertook to investigate a chemical weapons attack on the village of Birjinni. Birjinni is near Warmeli -- also a few hours' walk from Koreme in the direction of Turkey -- and although Koreme villagers did not pass through it during their flight, it had the main elements of chemical bombardment typically reported by survivors of the August 1988 Anfal campaign in the Dohuk region. Just as important, its survivors included eyewitnesses and relatives of the victims, and two of the victims were apparently buried soon after the attack in their original clothing.

---

[1] See generally Physicians for Human Rights, *Winds of Death: Iraq's Use of Poison Gas Against its Kurdish Population*, February 1989 ("Winds of Death"); A. Hay and G. Roberts, "The use of poison gas against the Iraqi Kurds: Analysis of bomb fragments, soil and wool samples," *Journal of the American Medical Association*, 1990;262:1065-1066; Hu, et al., "The Use of Chemical Weapons," *Journal of the American Medical Association*, 1989;262:640-643; Wolfe, "Chemical and Biological Warfare: Medical Effects and Consequences," 28 *McGill L.J.* 732 (1983).

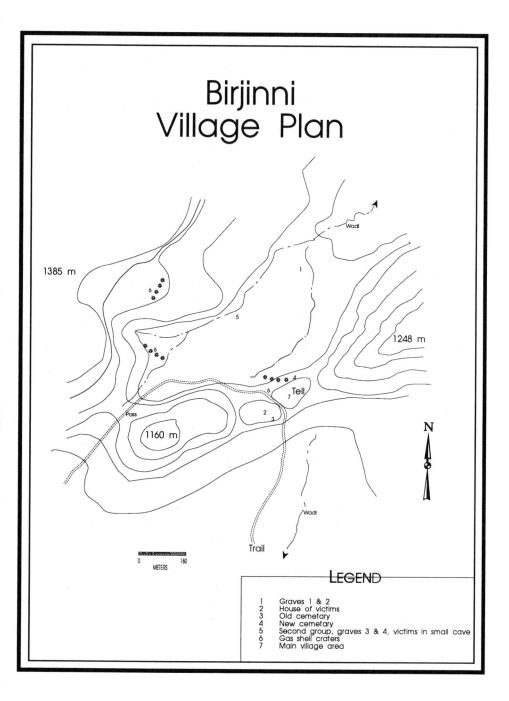

Birjinni
Village Plan

1385 m

6

6

5

1

Wadi

1248 m

4

6   Tell

7

Pass

2

3

1160 m

N

Trail

Wadi

0   180
METERS

LEGEND

1   Graves 1 & 2
2   House of victims
3   Old cemetary
4   New cemetary
5   Second group, graves 3 & 4, victims in small cave
6   Gas shell craters
7   Main village area

Birjinni's Isolation

Birjinni, before Anfal, was a small village of some 30 houses. The houses were made of stone and mud-brick, and there was a stone-and-cement mosque and a school built by the government in 1984. The village did not have electricity. It lies in the District of Zawita, Dohuk governorate, about an hour- and-a-half by car in good weather, plus a half hour walk up a mountain slope, from the town of Zawita.

The village occupies a narrow saddle and mountain pass along a chain of higher ridges between the cities of Zakho and Dohuk. It comprises a tell 10 meters high and 100 meters wide. On the north side of the village lies a low sloping terrace, consisting of about 0.3 hectares with orchards and limited farmland. (See Birjinni Village Plan.) Prior to the Anfal campaign, the villagers raised wheat, barley, lentils, watermelon, tomatoes, cucumbers, red peppers, apples, grapes, and pomegranates; they also kept flocks of sheep and goats. Temperatures are hot and dry in the summer, and villagers report that up to 2-3 meters of snow falls on the mountain saddle in winter. The slopes on each side of the saddle fall away steeply.

Two roads originally led to the village, one from Zawita and the second from Dohuk. The road to Dohuk was traditionally of great importance to the village, because the villagers went to the city to sell produce in the market. The villagers reported, however, that in 1980, the government closed the road as a counterinsurgency measure. Reportedly the government, concerned about peshmerga activity in the area, ordered the villagers to abandon Birjinni and move to a collective town near Dohuk. In addition, in the late 1970s and early 1980s, the government began bringing in Arabs from the south to regions in Dohuk to replace Kurds who had been removed from their lands to collective towns.

When the Birjinni and other villagers in the area refused to abandon their land, "the government cut off our village. They put up a line of military posts and checkpoints, and no one from our area was allowed to come through. We weren't allowed to go to Dohuk or to sell anything. If they caught people they beat them, and once in 1984 they executed seven men caught along the road." This was not the first time the road had been closed and the village isolated; villagers reported that it had been closed at various times, sometimes for several years, between the early 1960s and 1975.

There had long been active fighting between the army and peshmerga in the mountains and valleys around Birjinni. At various times during the 1980s, the peshmerga had bases within an hour's walk from Birjinni. Birjinni was fired upon with artillery and aerial bombardment off and on from "1975 through Anfal," although villagers reported that "no one was ever hit in those raids. We built ourselves shelters in the caves nearby on the hill. The army didn't dare come up here, there were too many peshmerga all around." Many of the village men were active peshmerga fighters in the mid to late 1980s, serving fifteen days on duty and fifteen days off. The peshmerga, villagers said, did not maintain a garrison in Birjinni itself.

The Chemical Weapons Attack

At dawn on August 25, 1988, Hassan, a farmer, was awake, but still inside his house in Birjinni. He lived there with his father and mother, his four brothers, and his wife and four children. He was preparing to go to the orchards that morning, unless bombing and artillery prevented him. There had been "a lot of bombing for days. We could see many aircraft passing all the time."

Hassan knew that the government and the peshmerga had each built up large ground forces to the north, but no battle had broken out. He had heard from numerous displaced persons passing through that the border with Turkey was closed, and that government soldiers were killing many who tried to cross. "They were being forced back into the lower valleys," he explained, "where they could be captured by the soldiers." He and other villagers tried to get more information from the KDP clandestine radio, but it was being jammed.

Hassan's wife was on the roof of the house at dawn and saw planes pass overhead. She saw them circle several times, but was not sure if they were observing the village or something else, because they were still far away. Hassan went outside to look, and reported a squadron of eight aircraft. Some of the villagers became frightened and went across the saddle to bomb shelters they had built on some ledges. Hassan and his family remained at home.

Shortly afterwards, the aircraft made a bombing run across the saddle on which the village sat, from east to west. Hassan reported seeing three planes drop four bombs each. Other surviving villagers agreed with his report; many had been watching the sky since early dawn, concerned that bombardment with conventional bombs was about to

35

begin. The bombs fell in three groups of four bombs, one group on the eastern edge of the village, and the other two on the western edge. Hassan's wife said they created a "tremendous noise"; her sister said the explosion was not like any of the other bombs that had been dropped on the village in previous years. Hassan said, by contrast, that the explosions were not as strong as other bombs dropped on the village. He reported seeing one group of four bombs fall "about 80 to 100 meters from the houses in the village."

Surviving villagers described the smoke rising from the bombs as "white, black, and then yellow, rising about 50 or 60 meters into the air in a column. Then the column began to break up and drift. It drifted down into the valley, and then passed through the village. Then we smelled the gas for the first time."

The smell of the gas was "pleasant, at first. It smelled of apples and something sweet." Several men said it smelled like "pesticides in the fields." Shortly thereafter, however, "it became bitter. It affected our eyes, and our mouths, and our skin. All of a sudden it was hard to breathe. Your breath wouldn't come. You couldn't breathe."[2]

The planes continued to fly overhead, said Hassan's sister-in-law, "in circles. They flew around and around. They watched us." And another village man added, "the [planes] flew very low, but they didn't fire at us with their machine guns." The planes reportedly stayed perhaps a half hour, until the main cloud of smoke had dispersed. Other villagers reported that the aircraft made other bombing sorties following the

---

[2] Survivor testimony does not establish what chemical agents were used at Birjinni -- blood agents, choking agents, blistering agents, or some combination -- although descriptions of symptoms suggest nerve agents. Iraq is thought to have used mustard gas, cyanide gas, and nerve agents. See Merkin, "Note: The Efficacy of Chemical-Arms Treaties in the Aftermath of the Iran-Iraq War," 9 *Boston v. Int'l. L.J.* 175 (Spring 1991) at note 74; *Time*, "Return of the Silent Killer," Aug. 22, 1988; *Newsweek*, "Letting a Genie Out of a Bottle," Sept. 19, 1988.

It is also not clear whether biological agents were ever used against the Kurds, although MEW has collected evidence independently confirming the conclusions of other researchers and intelligence agencies that Iraq in 1988 had both biological weapons and a biological weapons program. Letter of Human Rights Watch to Rolf Ekeus, United Nations Special Commission on Iraq, December 30, 1992.

chemical bombing, starting fires in the fields which, because it was late August, were dry and brown. There was burning everywhere.

The smoke from the chemical bombs, Hassan said, "settled into the lower land, it drifted down the valley toward the fields and the orchards. I took my family, three of my children and my wife, and we ran to higher ground. We went the other direction from the smoke." There was complete panic in the village; people ran in all directions, trying to escape. Families were separated, children were lost from their parents, and everyone, Hassan's wife said, "was trying to save themselves, each one himself, even the mothers of children, because they couldn't breathe."

But Hassan's father and mother, several brothers and a sister, stayed in the house, because "they didn't know what the smoke could do." When they understood what was happening, they ran from the house to an orchard in the ravine, "but it was deep in the valley. The smoke followed them, and there they were overcome." Hassan and his wife realized that one of their four children, Dejwar, a boy of five years, was missing. Dejwar had gone with his grandfather to the orchard in the ravine, and not up the hill with his father and mother.

After about half an hour, Hassan and other survivors on higher ground thought it was safe to come back down to the village. The planes had flown off, and Hassan took that as a good sign. Nearby the house, however, they found Hassan's mother and twelve-year-old sister lying on the ground, overcome by the gas. Survivors took them and the other injured people to the spring and began to wash them with water. The mother and sister had similar symptoms, family members said; their hands and legs were paralyzed, they "were trembling and shaking all over, especially in their limbs." Hassan's wife and sister-in-law tried to get them to swallow water, but "they couldn't. Their throats were burning, and they were vomiting. My mother whispered, 'I think there's a hole in my head'." Within several hours after exposure to the smoke, both the mother and sister went blind, according to family members; the condition lasted several weeks for each of them.

Hassan went down from the village and found his father, a man "more than sixty years old," and his son Dejwar lying dead just outside the orchard. He could find no marks on the bodies that he could see, "it was like they were sleeping, except their faces were blue." His two brothers were also found dead in the small cave where they had taken cover together.

37

These four -- the grandfather, Hasan Saleh Hasan, born c. 1930; Hasan's two brothers, Hakim Hasan Saleh, born 1964, and Kurdi Hasan Saleh, born 1965; and Hasan's son Dejwar Hamid Hasan, born 1983 -- were the total dead from the chemical attack on August 25, 1988, according to village survivors.[3] There were "many injured, some more seriously than others," villagers said, but no tally was made.[4]

The Aftermath of the Attack

Those who could fled Birjinni within hours of the attack. They feared the planes would return and that government soldiers would arrive shortly. They understood that this was a wholly different kind of attack; whereas, in earlier episodes, they had only to protect themselves from artillery and bombardment, relatively sheltered in their remote mountain home, the gas attack was obviously a prelude to something new. Looking down into the valleys from their mountain saddle, they could see large groups of peasants trying to flee to Turkey, as the villagers from Koreme, Warmeli, and numerous other places sought to do. The peshmerga did not seem able to fight a holding action to allow the civilians to retreat behind them. The enormity of the government action and the use of chemicals as a weapon of terror had thrown everything into confusion.

Not everyone was able to go to Turkey, however. Hassan's mother, injured in the chemical attack and by now blinded and partly paralyzed, her muscles "fluttering like an insect's," was unable to undertake the arduous trip. She started out with the others, her son said, but could not go on and turned back with other villagers, including some men who later disappeared in government custody.

---

[3] Galbraith & Van Hollen, based on interviews in Turkey, list 80 dead from chemical attacks on Birjinni. Their report apparently refers to a wider geographic area than just the village of Birjinni proper, which is very small.

[4] Iraqi government denials that it used chemical weapons against the Kurds are patently false. Middle East Watch has viewed video records of chemical gas attacks on Kurdish villages, shot by government forces themselves in 1982. For a general account of the U.S. response to chemical weapons attacks against the Kurds, see Deanne E. Maynard, "Iraq: United States Response to the Alleged Use of Chemical Weapons Against the Kurds," 2 *Harvard Human Rights Yearbook* 179 (Spring 1989).

The fleeing villagers left the bodies unburied, so great was their hurry. They brought the grandfather and little boy's bodies further down the valley to the bottom of the orchard and left them there. The two brothers were left in the cave where they had succumbed. Government soldiers apparently arrived in the village two days later and subsequently buried the bodies of the grandfather and little boy near where they had been left. They were buried in their clothes, without the performance of Islamic ritual. The two brothers were not buried at all, but instead the soldiers left them in the cave in large nylon or plastic wrappings.

In 1991, shortly after the March 1991 Kurdish uprising, a peshmerga from Koreme, whose sister was married to one of the dead brothers, ventured up to Birjinni. He found the skeletons of the two brothers in the plastic or nylon sacks, and buried them at the cave. He found the unmarked graves of the grandfather and son, partially digging up one body to be sure, and then covering it back over. The soldiers took custody of the villagers who had either returned or never left, removing them first to the fort in Dohuk, and later to the collective camp at Beharke near Erbil. An unknown number of the village men, who had stayed behind rather than flee to Turkey, disappeared after being taken to the Dohuk fort.

Those who went on to Turkey traveled by night. On the afternoon of the attack, they went to a nearby mountain and hid until dark. Then they moved slowly and cautiously across the hills and ravines between Birjinni and the mountains marking the border. There were "thousands and thousands of other people on the roads," and in the end, it was perhaps the fact that so many people were fleeing that enabled them to slip through. Even given the size of the government force assigned to capture the Kurdish villagers, the number fleeing was so great that some got through the Iraqi army lines.[5] But it took the Birjinni villagers three days to get to Turkey. Iraqi soldiers shot at them and shelled the area. The survivors saw the bodies of people killed by Iraqi soldiers as they tried to flee, and at least two of their own villagers were killed by mortar fire; as "soon as [the soldiers] saw us, they shot at us. I don't know how we could have surrendered to them, they just shot at us."

---

[5] See *Int'l. Herald Tribune*, "Refugee Kurds Say Iraqi Poison Gas May Be Killing More in Homeland, "Sept. 7, 1988 ("...Iraqi troops now effectively sealing much of the Turkish border..."); *Int'l. Herald Tribune*, "Turkey Says Iraqis Have Blocked Routes Used By Kurdish Refugees," Sept. 7, 1988.

Still, many did surrender, including families from Birjinni and "the men from those families, we don't know where they are today, they disappeared."

At the border, the Birjinni villagers were met by units of the Turkish army. Turkish soldiers took them into custody and, according to the villagers, planned to repatriate them to the Iraqi army.[6] They watched others being repatriated, but for unknown reasons, the Birjinni villagers were taken to a refugee camp and given asylum. At the camp, Turkish physicians examined their chemical weapons injuries, but gave them no specific treatment, villagers said.[7] The sister who was blind regained her eyesight after several months; her muscles continued to have spasms, and she suffered from partial paralysis and "weakness."

The Birjinni villagers remained in the refugee camp at Diyarbakir, Turkey until the uprising in March 1991, when they came back across the border. They returned to their village and discovered that it, like so many others, had been methodically destroyed in its entirety. The school, mosque and stone houses had been dynamited to rubble; the mud houses had been scraped to the ground. Nothing remained. Landmines were placed around the village to deter its inhabitants from returning.

They went to live as refugees in a collective town near the main Dohuk highway, going up to the mountains to begin replanting the crops and the orchards for a few days at a time, walking the six hours in each direction from the busstop on the main Zawita road to the village.

---

[6] For reports of forcible repatriation by the Turkish government, in violation of international law governing refugees and asylum, see *Int'l. Herald Tribune*, "Taking in the Fleeing Kurds: Turkey Treads a Difficult Path," Sept. 8, 1988; *Sydney Morning Herald*, "Ankara Shuts Door on Kurds Fleeing Iraq," Sept. 9, 1988. Turkey, despite certain forced repatriations, reluctantly accepted over 60,000 refugees (including the Birjinni villagers) on humanitarian grounds although it refused to acknowledge the Kurds' rights to the Protection of the Refugee Convention.

[7] The Turkish government rejected the claim that chemical weapons were used on the Kurds. *N.Y. Times*, "Turkey Opposes an Inquiry into Poison Gas Issue," Sept. 15, 1988. Turkish government doctors claimed to find no medical evidence of chemical weapons against the Kurds, and instead suggested exposure and poor diet. *N.Y. Times*, "Kurd's Symptoms: Gas or Poor Diet?" Sept. 12, 1988.

Since then, the apple trees have blossomed, despite an unusually harsh winter in 1991-92, and some of the grape vines and pomegranates have been replanted. By June 1992, the wheat was ready for harvest, although landmines in the fields presented a consistent danger.

Investigations By the Forensic Team

Members of the forensic team visited Birjinni in the company of villagers on June 1, 7, and 10, 1992. The team's activities, detailed in Appendices 1 and 2, divide into four types: Taking the survivor testimony summarized above; archaeological investigation and mapping of the village as it existed prior to destruction; investigation and sampling of the sites where chemical bombs were reported to have fallen; and exhumation of the remains of two victims of the chemical weapons attack.

Birjinni village. The team archaeologist undertook to map and survey the village to establish the structures that existed prior to its destruction (see Birjinni Village Plan). His investigations demonstrated that the village consisted of approximately 40 houses, as described above, with two stone and concrete structures reported by villagers to have been the school and mosque. All buildings had been destroyed; it was not possible on the basis of physical evidence to state with certainty the year of destruction, but the vegetation growth and other evidence was consistent with the former inhabitants' report that the village had been destroyed in 1988.

The school and mosque, as identified by villagers, had evidently been destroyed from the inside, with explosives aimed to implode structures rather than explode them, given the configuration of rubble located within the interior of the building site. The buildings had collapsed upon themselves. These conclusions are consistent with eyewitness accounts of the destruction of cement buildings in other villages.[8] They are also consistent with the account in "The End of

---

[8] An Assyrian Christian priest interviewed by MEW in June 1992 gave the following account of the destruction of his church in the village of Bakhtoma in April 1987: "I was the last one to pray in the church. After finishing my prayer, I took out the furniture to take to Dohuk. It was a very sad day. The Iraqi soldiers and members of engineering units in the Iraqi army put the equivalent of one kilogram of TNT in each of the corners of the church; then after five minutes they blew it up. They destroyed it completely and they demolished

41

Anfal" of special demolition teams detailed to undertake the "destruction and removal of the remnants of the saboteurs and their premises."[9] The remainder of the houses had been razed down to their foundations, in a fashion indicating the use of earth moving and scraping equipment.

The chemical weapons bomb sites. The team archaeologist also investigated the sites where villagers indicated chemical bombs had fallen (see Birjinni Village Plan). He found three clusters of four airborne canisters, each spaced around the edge of the village terrace. Four of these bomb craters, along the western edge of the terrace and about 700 meters from the village, were examined in detail, while the locations of the other eight craters were visually confirmed.

The four craters examined in detail consisted of low conical depressions 2.2 meters across and 0.6 to 1.2 meters deep. Fragments of the bombs were found lying immediately beside and in the craters. In two instances they consisted of an iron outer envelope that was heavily rusted, an aluminum inner canister, a heavy lid labelled "Top" in English, a spout in the lid, and twisted tail fins. The fragments near each crater in those two instances were sizable: approximately 1 meter by 0.5 meter by 0.5 meter, and approximately 10 kilos in weight.

Soil samples were collected from the craters and scraped from inside a canister. At the time of writing, laboratory analysis of the samples is still underway.[10] The four craters were spaced on a straight line about thirty meters apart, consistent with survivor accounts that they had been dropped from low altitude by aircraft heading in a westerly direction.

Exhumations of chemical weapons victims. Under the direction of the forensic team's scientific head and chief anthropologist, the skeletal remains of two of the four apparent victims of the chemical attack were exhumed. The forensic team was told that these two skeletons were those of the grandfather and the small boy who had died in the attack. The skeletons of the other two victims, buried in the cave, were not exhumed.

---

every single house in the village."

[9] "The End of Anfal" at 33.

[10] Laboratory analysis is being conducted in the United Kingdom. Thus far, it has shown only that the clothing contains no residues of mustard gas.

Exhumation of the two skeletons confirmed that one was that of an old man, approximately sixty years old. Relatives identified him as the grandfather on the basis of artifacts and clothing found with the skeleton in the grave. The second skeleton was that of a young boy, approximately five years old. He was identified as the grandson on the basis of clothing. Forensic examination of the two skeletons was limited to determining whether there was any sign of trauma or perimortem violence that might contradict the account of the villagers that the two decedents were overcome by chemical weapons. No indications contrary to death by chemical agents were found. The skeletons were then reburied in new graves in accordance with Islamic ritual.

Conclusions concerning the chemical weapons attack. The forensic team found nothing in the evidence of the exhumation and the archaeological investigation that was inconsistent with the account of the chemical weapons attack given by village witnesses. On the contrary, the lack of trauma to either skeleton supports the villagers' account. The physical evidence of the canisters, although lacking physical evidence of the specific chemical agents deployed apparently by reason of time, chemical and weather-related deterioration, also supports the villagers' account.

Iraq has admitted using chemical weapons during these years, and the international community has concluded there is no question that Iraq used chemical weapons against Iran in the Iran-Iraq War, and against Kurdish civilians in the late 1980s.[11] Moreover, the account of the Birjinni villagers is consistent with numerous other confirmed accounts of chemical weapons in the area, and is substantially the same as the

---

[11] Indirect official admissions of chemical weapons use by Iraq include, for example, a news conference in Baghdad in September 1988 in which the then-Iraqi Minister of Defense, Adnan Khairallah, while stating that the policy of Iraq was not to use chemical weapons, added that "if this is the rule, then each rule has an exception." *Int'l. Herald Tribune*, "Iraq Suggests Gas Use Is Government's Right," Sept. 16, 1988. United Nations investigators had concluded in 1988 that Iraq's use of chemical weapons in the Iran-Iraq War was "intense and frequent." *Int'l. Herald Tribune*, "UN Is Asked to Check Reports on Kurds," Sept. 14, 1988; among the U.N. reports, see 43 U.N. SCOR, U.N. Doc. S/19832 (1988) (one of four 1988 reports). The U.S. concluded that Iraq used chemical weapons against the Kurds in 1988; see generally Maynard, *Harvard Human Rights Yearbook 179*, op cit.

account concerning Birjinni appearing in Galbraith & Van Hollen, finding that Birjinni was attacked with chemical weapons. Birjinni villagers, interviewed by PHR investigators in Turkey in 1988, gave the same account.

Accordingly, notwithstanding that the laboratory analysis of physical samples of chemical agents has not been completed, and taking into account eyewitness reports by the villagers, the forensic team is of the opinion that the village of Birjinni was attacked by chemical weapons on or about August 25, 1988; that some or all of the craters investigated by the team archaeologist were made by chemical weapons bombs; and that the skeletal remains exhumed by the forensic team were those of chemical weapons victims.

The Firing Squad at Koreme

In keeping with Kurdish tradition, many -- probably most -- Koreme men, went armed into the mountains when the village fled. Some were armed with up-to-date Kalashnikov AK-47 assault rifles, other with older weapons, including shotguns and old M-1 rifles. Some carried pistols. In some cases, these weapons were obtained through peshmerga service.

Returning to surrender at Koreme, some men hid their weapons in the dirt and brush in the mountains, fearing that soldiers might open fire on them from a distance if they saw weapons. They also knew the weapons would be taken from them in any case if they surrendered, so they had nothing to lose by hiding their weapons and hoping to return for them in the future. Other men, however, kept their weapons as they returned to Koreme, and when they were met by soldiers, just outside the village, put their hands "high into the air." The soldiers immediately separated the villagers into three groups -- women and children, old men, and young and adult men. They disarmed those men who were armed, and searched them and the other men to find any other weapons.

The squad of soldiers -- estimates of the number of soldiers ranged from several dozen to over a hundred -- was accompanied by National Defense Battalions units, estimated to number in the hundreds. The National Defense Battalions led the remaining animals away; the villagers did not see them again. It was afternoon on August 28, 1988; estimates of the time range from early afternoon to early evening. The number of villagers captured by the soldiers in this incident was somewhere between 150 and 300.

The Firing Squad

The Iraqi soldiers were led by two lieutenants, reportedly both appearing to be in their twenties. They were Arabs, spoke Arabic to each other and to the villagers, some of whom spoke Arabic as well as Kurdish, and communicated with their commander in Mengish by walkie-talkie. One of the lieutenants separated a group of village men, finally reduced to thirty three, from the group of young and adult men. Survivor reports differed as to whether these men had all been carrying weapons on their return to Koreme; some said that all had weapons, while others said some did but others did not.

Whether or not all of the men and boys taken aside were carrying weapons when they were captured -- it is irrelevant to the legal assessment of the crime that followed -- survivor accounts are uniform that these men were made to form a line. A lieutenant told them to sit down, and they did so, squatting on their heels rather than sitting in the dirt. The other villagers, including those men not singled out, were led away behind the hill near the partly-ruined village schoolhouse. Women and men screamed and cried out for their loved ones as they were taken away, and the soldiers and militiamen tried to quiet them down.

"We just want to ask them some questions," a soldier reportedly said to the wife of one of the detained men. "Why do you think something's going to happen?" One of the lieutenants went down the row of men, pulling aside those he apparently thought too young. An argument developed over whether one boy was twelve or thirteen; he was finally allowed to go free. One boy, who tried to stand with his father, was taken out of the line. Another young teenager, holding his baby sister in his arms, was also taken out of the line. By the time the boys had been pulled aside, there were thirty three men and teenage boys left in line. No one was asked for identity cards or other papers. The villagers near the schoolhouse, behind the hill, could no longer see the men, but they continued to call out to them, weeping and wailing despite the assurances of the soldiers.

The thirty three detained men, too, wept and pleaded for the lives, although the soldiers insisted that nothing would happen to them. One of the lieutenants offered them cigarettes and water; meanwhile, some twelve to fifteen soldiers had taken up positions facing the line. Some of them, too, told the men that nothing would happen. The commander, they said, was going to call for orders from Mengish, so they would know what questions to ask.

Shortly thereafter, one of the lieutenants called on his walkie-talkie for orders from his commander in Mengish. He reported capturing "armed subversives" and asked for instructions. The men in the line could not hear the reply from Mengish. However, according to survivors, as soon as he put down the walkie-talkie, he turned around to the soldiers facing the men and shouted at them to shoot.

The soldiers opened fire at the line of thirty three squatting men from a distance of about 5-10 meters. (See Plan of Koreme Execution Site and Appendix III.) The soldiers were armed, according to execution survivors, with Kalashnikov AK-47 rifles, and they sprayed bullets along the line. It was not possible to determine how long the firing went on or how many rounds were fired. Some survivors reported that the firing went on for several seconds. The forensic team, sweeping the whole execution site, recovered 124 cartridge cases, although these do not establish the total rounds fired. Sixty-three cases were obtained at the site surface and were piece-plotted, allowing forensic analysis of the number of weapons and their movement during the execution.

Ballistics and forensic experts examining the cartridge cases and their location on behalf of MEW/PHR have determined that there were at least seven individual firearms used in the execution.[1] The firearms were all semi-automatic or fully-automatic 7.62 x 39mm caliber. Physical evidence strongly indicates only a single event involving the firing of over 100 rounds of 7.62mm caliber ammunition. Of the seven shooters at minimum taking part in the execution, at least one fired thirty seven rounds, at a minimum, as determined by forensic examination of firing pin imprints on the cartridge cases. Assuming a full AK-47 or similar weapon magazine of 30 rounds, that particular individual apparently reloaded at least once during the execution. This same shooter, in addition to reloading at least once during the execution, also moved closest to the victim line compared with the other shooters, on the basis of the dispersal of piece-plotted cartridge cases.

Some men were killed immediately by rifle fire. Others were wounded, and a few were missed altogether. Remarkably, given the volume of firing, there were six survivors out of the thirty three men and boys. After the soldiers stopped shooting, several soldiers approached the line of slumped bodies on orders of the lieutenant and fired additional individual rounds as a coup de grace. The soldiers then left the execution site, without burying the bodies or otherwise touching them, according to survivors who lay among the corpses.

---

[1] See Appendix 3, Report on Firearms Identification of the Koreme Execution Site for the complete analysis of firearms and ballistics. MEW/PHR are grateful to Douglas D. Scott, Ph.D., who carried out this analysis.

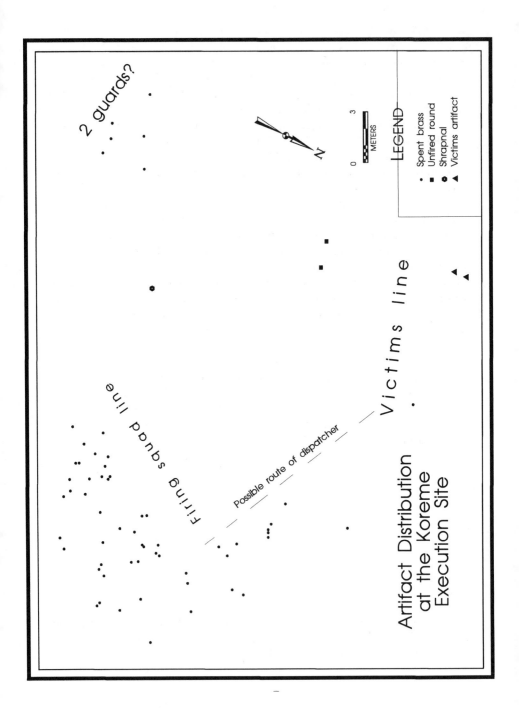

2 guards?

N

LEGEND

• Spent brass
■ Unfired round
⬢ Shrapnal
▲ Victims artifact

0   3
▬▬▬▬▬
METERS

Firing squad line

Possible route of dispatcher

Victims line

Artifact Distribution
at the Koreme
Execution Site

Survivor testimony is clear that the execution was ordered by superior officers at the Mengish headquarters, several kilometers away. Although the lieutenants in charge did not organize a regular execution with any formal procedures other than having the thirty three men squat in line, neither were they surprised by the order. Nor did their men seem surprised by the order, when given, to open fire. Executions of this kind appear to have been contemplated as part of the military operation, even if the reason for selecting these particular men and not others is unclear.[2]

On the evidence, it therefore appears this was not a case of a local officer acting beyond the scope of his command. The local officers proceeded on orders from above. Moreover, other units, with other commanders and other headquarters, proceeded in the same manner. This was an atrocity of a systematic character, part of the Anfal campaign, and carried out according to the orders of the day.

---

[2] Koreme was not the only Dohuk village where such executions took place; a similar execution of seven men from the village of Mergatou, also took place in late August 1988, as part of the same Anfal operation. The surviving witnesses from Mergatou, illiterate wives of the executed men, could not give an exact date, although they knew it was in late August. They, too, were captured as they fled the Anfal attack. Their village was much smaller and had fewer young or adult men.

According to relatives of the sole survivor, interviewed by MEW/PHR, who disappeared later from a hospital where he was taken for wounds suffered at the time of the execution, the squad leader received orders by walkie-talkie to execute the men of the village. He did not do so, and instead brought all the villagers to the local headquarters, where women, children, and the elderly were being put on trucks and sent to forts. According to the survivor's account to his relatives, the squad leader was rebuked by his commander and, the same evening, was sent back to the village with the eight men to execute them in the place where he had originally been ordered to do. Of the eight, later seven died, and one survived, wounded, until he was forcibly disappeared.

The Twenty Seven Dead

The identities of the twenty seven men and boys who died in front of the firing squad at Koreme on August 28, 1988 are as follows:

Name	Age	Village
1. Huseen-Kader, Sagvan	16	Koreme
2. Huseen-Kader, Shaaban	14	Koreme
3. Mohamed-Abdullah, Khalil	43	Koreme
4. Khalil-Mohamed, Adnan	13	Koreme
5. Othman-Mostafa, Morad	19	Koreme
6. Mostafa-Saleh, Zahir	39	Koreme
7. Mostafa-Saleh, Zober	37-38	Koreme
8. Hamdy-Mostafa, Chaban	25	Koreme
9. Khalil-Mohamed, Abdulsalam	26	Koreme
10. Abdullah-Kader, Hameed	23	Koreme
11. Abdullah-Kader, Sedeek	17	Koreme
12. Hasen-Merza, Salam	20	Koreme
13. Hasen-Merza, Saleh	16	Koreme
14. Mohamed-Fatah Fatah	15	Koreme
15. Huseen-Omer, Abdulrahman	38	Koreme
16. Soleman-Esmaeel, Haje	38	Koreme
17. Mostafa-Esmaeel, Khaled	25	Koreme
18. Mostafa-Esmaeel, Salah	23	Koreme
19. Shareef-Fatah, Akram	34	Chalkey
20. Shareef-Fatah, Abdulsata	24	Chalkey
21. Shareef-Fatah, Mosa	18	Chalkey
22. Hasen-Taha, Fadel	19	Chalkey
23. Jaafer-Taha, Rasheed	19	Chalkey
24. Yacoob-Kasem, Mohamed	38	Chalkey
25. Hakeem-Yacoob, Morad	24	Chalkey
26. Yacoob-Kasem, Ahmed	39	Chalkey
27. Abdulkader-Fatah, Norey	34	Chalkey

There were six survivors of a total of ee men and boys in front of the firing squad; their full names cannot be released for reasons of their personal security, except for the name of one survivor who was later captured and disappeared by Iraqi forces at Dohuk fort: Abdulkader-Fatah, Fatah, age unknown, of Chalkey village.

50

The mean age of the victims was 25.5 years. Ten of the twenty seven dead were under 20 years old. Five were 16 years old or younger, and the youngest was 13.

How Did the Six Survive?

Despite the conclusion that the execution was not an isolated act of indiscipline, it also appears that the soldiers performing the execution were not as diligent as they might have been. The fact that there were six survivors out of 33 men, some of whom were not hit at all, despite having been sprayed with automatic weapons fire by a seven or more men from a distance of 5-10 meters, suggests that some of the soldiers fired over the heads of the squatting men.

Even the coups de grace appear to have been unsystematic. One survivor reported feeling the bullet of the coup de grace go directly past his ear, but miss him altogether.

Another survivor, Aba, who was born in 1954, reported that in the initial round of bullets, he was hit in the left leg. The force of the bullet blew him over backwards from his squatting position, shattering bones in his leg, and caused him to roll down a slope. "I fell into a stony ravine, among some boulders," he said. No soldiers pursued him down the hill but, he said, they shot at him as he rolled. He said he was "partly visible and partly hidden by grass and stones." Aba said that he remained on his back at the ravine bottom for twenty-four hours. Occasionally through the night, he said, soldiers up the hill "would shoot at me. But no one came after me, because they thought I was dead."

On the afternoon of the following day, Aba said, soldiers finally came down the hill and found that he was alive, because "I tried to stand up." The soldiers "spoke to me, but I didn't understand, because it was Arabic," he said. They called by radio to the commander in Mengish, he said, and "I understood enough Arabic to know they said 'Calling Mengish, calling Mengish'. I thought they were going to finish me off." Instead, however, "about 20 Jash [National Defense Battalions] took me up the hill to an ambulance" and from there to the clinic in Mengish. Aba spent two days in the hospital at Mengish, where he was treated by a doctor who "only washed the wound out with water, and I have a bad limp still and can't be a farmer anymore."

After being released from the hospital, Aba was taken to the Dohuk fort where thousands of other Kurdish villagers, including those from Koreme, were being held. He had no explanation as to why he was

51

not taken away from Dohuk Fort, when almost all other adult Kurdish males were removed and disappeared in the hands of Iraqi security forces.

The other five survivors appear to have lived because the bullets missed altogether, or because they were only lightly wounded. As the bodies were not buried immediately, and so the survivors were able to crawl away to hide when the soldiers had returned to their base up the hill.

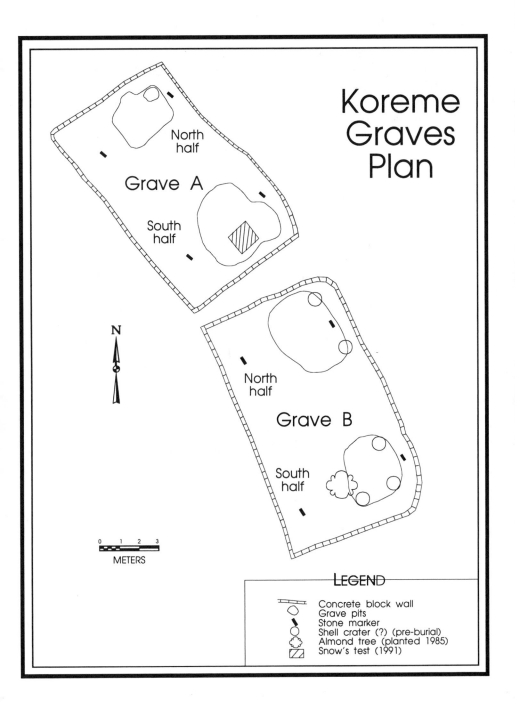

Koreme
Graves
Plan

North
half

Grave A

South
half

North
half

Grave B

South
half

N

0 1 2 3
METERS

LEGEND

Concrete block wall
Grave pits
Stone marker
Shell crater (?) (pre-burial)
Almond tree (planted 1985)
Snow's test (1991)

Burying the Bodies

All the remaining inhabitants of Koreme -- between 150 and 300 persons, according to different accounts -- were removed from the village that same day, without being allowed to bury their dead. They were taken by soldiers and the National Defense Battalions to the fort and other installations in Mengish.

The bodies left at Koreme putrefied rapidly in the August and September sun. Kurds allowed to remain in Mengish reported that soldiers began to complain of the smell after a week or so even from their post further up the hill above the village. Somewhere between a week and three weeks after the massacre -- there are no available eyewitnesses -- Iraqi soldiers or the National Defense Battalions reportedly buried the massacre victims in two shallow pits, each containing two separate pits measuring approximately 2 x 2 meters. (See Koreme Graves Plan.)

The absence of identity cards or personal valuables on the bodies when disinterred by the forensic team indicates that someone had stripped the bodies of these items. The bodies were likely looted of these items before they were buried in the common pits where the forensic team disinterred them, since there was no indication that the bodies had been disturbed once covered over. It is logical to assume, though not proven, that since soldiers and the National Defense Battalions were the only persons allowed in the area between the date of the massacre and burial, soldiers, militiamen, or both, were responsible for looting the bodies.

Three of the four graves (Graves B-S, A-S, and B-N) contained earth disturbances, appearing to be artillery shell craters, from which shrapnel fragments were recovered. The artillery holes may have provided a convenient starting point for gravedigging. The four graves run along a line about 10 meters northwest of the line where the Koreme men were killed.

The graves were not disturbed between the date of burial and the forensic team's exhumation, so far as the forensic team was able to determine. One villager, an elderly man, who was sometimes given permission to leave the Beharke camp where the survivors were ultimately taken and who had sons in the graves, came to Koreme in 1990 and made a low wall of cinder blocks around each of the two pits containing the four graves.

54

Koreme gravesite with villagers looking on.
© Susan Meiselas, Magnum Photos, Inc.

Middle East Watch and Physicians for Human Rights forensic team members (from Chile and Argentina) excavating a skeleton from Koreme village with the assistance of villagers.
© Susan Meiselas, Magnum Photos, Inc.

Excavation of Erbil gravesite.
© Susan Meiselas, Magnum Photos, Inc.

Preparing a Koreme skeleton for exhumation and laboratory
identification.
© Susan Meiselas, Magnum Photos, Inc.

Dr. Clyde Snow with the international forensic team examining a
skeleton in the Dohuk Hospital morgue.
© Susan Meiselas, Magnum Photos, Inc.

The Chilean member of the forensic team, Isabel Reveco, cleans a
Koreme skeleton as villagers look on.
© Susan Meiselas, Magnum Photos, Inc.

Village woman beside the exhumed skeleton of her brother at the
Koreme gravesite.
© Susan Meiselas, Magnum Photos, Inc.

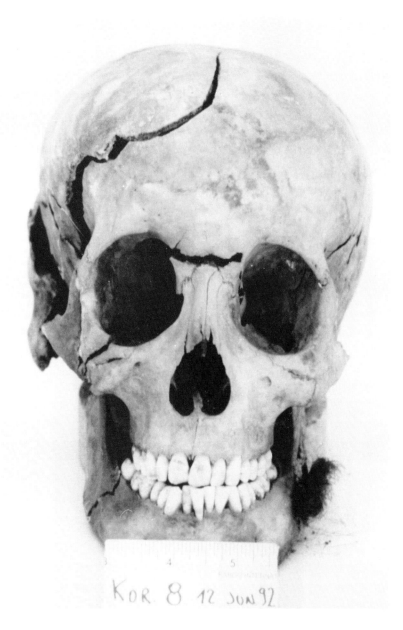

Skull of Koreme victim.
© Mercedes Doretti

Reburial of the skeletons at Koreme.
© Mercedes Doretti

The village cemetery at Jeznikam-Beharke.
© Susan Meiselas, Magnum Photos, Inc.

The Forensic Team's Exhumation

The forensic team exhumed the two grave pits following standard archaeological and forensic procedures.[3] Each grave pit was roughly 2x2 meters. The pits contained disturbances and shrapnel supporting that they had originally been artillery shell craters. A floating grid system was established for documenting the exhumation work; artifacts, clothing, and skeletal remains were recorded on standard field inventory forms and skeletons were removed from the pit in anatomical order. Evidence of trauma to each skeleton was noted on a skeletal checklist form as each bone was removed. Skeletons and other evidence were removed to the Dohuk Hospital Morgue where the forensic team undertook reconstruction and identification of each of the twenty seven skeletons.

The forensic team found that each of the twenty seven skeletons were male, ranging in age from early teens to middle 40s. Each of the twenty seven died from gunshot wounds. The primary target of the gunshots appeared to be the trunk of the body, with some indications that the executioners were aiming on a downward slant toward the front of the victims, although the pattern of wounds suggests that some victims were shot in the back or side as they involuntarily tried to twist or turn away as the volleys began. These findings are consistent both with survivor oral testimony and with ballistic analysis that the executioners were standing in a line facing a line of squatting victims.

Clothing, artifacts, and medical and dental testimony enabled the forensic team to positively identify each of the twenty seven victims.

---

[3] See Appendices 1-3 for discussion of exhumation methods, analysis, and results.

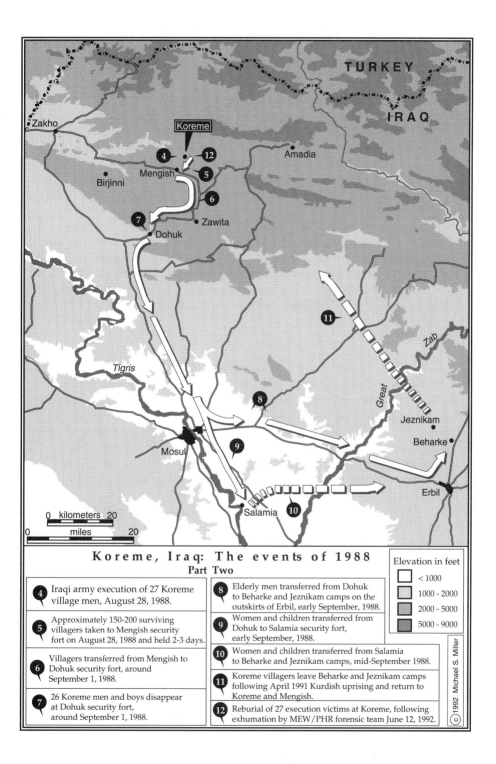

Koreme, Iraq: The events of 1988
Part Two

Elevation in feet
- ☐ < 1000
- 1000 - 2000
- 2000 - 5000
- 5000 - 9000

4 Iraqi army execution of 27 Koreme village men, August 28, 1988.

5 Approximately 150-200 surviving villagers taken to Mengish security fort on August 28, 1988 and held 2-3 days.

6 Villagers transferred from Mengish to Dohuk security fort, around September 1, 1988.

7 26 Koreme men and boys disappear at Dohuk security fort, around September 1, 1988.

8 Elderly men transferred from Dohuk to Beharke and Jeznikam camps on the outskirts of Erbil, early September, 1988.

9 Women and children transferred from Dohuk to Salamia security fort, early September, 1988.

10 Women and children transferred from Salamia to Beharke and Jeznikam camps, mid-September 1988.

11 Koreme villagers leave Beharke and Jeznikam camps following April 1991 Kurdish uprising and return to Koreme and Mengish.

12 Reburial of 27 execution victims at Koreme, following exhumation by MEW/PHR forensic team June 12, 1992.

©1992 Michael S. Miller

Detention and Disappearance

Although they saw nothing, the villagers taken behind the hill near the schoolhouse heard shots and knew what they meant. Soldiers and militiamen forcibly prevented them from running back to their men, who by now were receiving the coup de grace. Men and women "both wept," said one widow, "and the children screamed for their fathers."

The surviving villagers were mostly women, children and elderly, numbering between 150 and 300. Although they were hungry and thirsty after their long excursion through the mountains, the soldiers hustled them down the hill on foot from Koreme to the district capital of Mengish. Mengish, a town of a few thousand, with electricity, running water, and some paved roads, also had, like all provincial towns, a military fortress, to which the Koreme survivors were taken. It was filled to bursting with thousands of other Kurdish villagers; some Koreme villagers reported having been held in the Mengish school.

Mengish Fort

Mengish fort, a cement and stone building, contained a warren of dark cells and some interior courtyards. Jammed with captured Kurds, it offered appalling sanitation, food and water. Most villagers reported that they received no food whatsoever during the two to four days they were there; a few reported receiving one or two pieces of Kurdish flat bread. One man reported being kept in solitary confinement in a classroom of Mengish school for two days without food or water, although on the second day someone outside the school threw bread through the window and then ran away.

Water, too, was not generally distributed. Many people went without any for several days. Others received a little bit when some barrels of hot, sun-heated water were placed in the courtyard. It was not enough to go around, and in any case, since most people had nothing to carry it with, they went with very little or without.

Dohuk Fort

After a few days in the Mengish fort, the Koreme villagers were gradually moved in small groups to the enormous fortress at the provincial capital of Dohuk, a journey of about one hour.

The young and adult men were transported separately from their wives and other family members. Aba, one of the men who survived execution at Koreme, was one of those transported to Dohuk fort, although with his wounded leg disinfected but not set, he could hardly walk. But, he said, "I had no fever, so I knew I wouldn't get gangrene and I knew I would live, if they didn't kill me."

At Dohuk fort, according to Koreme villagers, conditions were scarcely better than at Mengish, even though many villagers remained at Dohuk for several weeks. Some food and water was distributed, but it rarely amounted to more than a piece of bread every other day, handed out negligently. Water supplies remained limited to a few barrels of hot water placed in courtyards that were unsanitary and insufficient to meet drinking needs.

Some pregnant women were said to have miscarried, a result physicians confirmed was unsurprising in the circumstances, given the women's stress, declining nutrition and, particularly, dehydration. There was no report of any medical care; one woman who asked for a doctor was told by a soldier that "the Kurds have been brought here to die." MEW/PHR received testimony of similar remarks made by Iraqi soldiers to detained Kurds on many occasions.

A woman was reported by women of Koreme to have died in premature labor in the fort; her husband, they said, was not with her.

Children suffered especially. Some reportedly died in the fort, while others appear to have been so weakened that, in combination with the subsequent adverse conditions of the camps at Jeznikam and Beharke, near Erbil, to which they were subsequently transferred, they rapidly succumbed. Nursing mothers, too, faced special difficulties. One boy, who had been pushed out of the execution line at Koreme by a lieutenant, said that when "we reached Dohuk fort, my mother's milk dried up." The infant sister that his mother was nursing eventually died in Beharke camp.

There are virtually no differences in the accounts given to MEW/PHR of Mengish and Dohuk with respect to these essentials of food, water, and sanitation, not only by Koreme villagers, but also by people from other villages imprisoned there. Moreover, the accounts are consistent with the treatment of Kurdish villagers captured and detained in other forts at the time of the Anfal campaign in the region of northern Iraqi Kurdistan.

The Disappearances

While in custody in Dohuk, approximately twenty-six young and adult Koreme men disappeared at the hands of Iraqi security agents and soldiers.

According to family members who were also held captive in Dohuk fort, the disappearances took place in two separate sweeps. Young and adult men were generally held separately from their families in the fort, although some were allowed to mingle on occasion. Some of the men and teenage boys "were beaten up by the guards. I don't know why," said the mother of a disappeared young man. Other Koreme villagers reported more serious physical abuse, including systematic beatings of men who were hung by wires.

The first sweep of which Koreme villagers were aware took place on the second day after most villagers had been moved from Mengish to Dohuk (other sweeps, resulting in other disappearances, were reported by others imprisoned in Dohuk fort). Guards circulated among the captives; they did not ask for identity cards or documents, nor did they work from any apparent list. Rather, they seemed simply to be judging men and boys by their age. According to surviving family members, if a man looked "too young" or a boy "too old," then he was taken away. The wife of a Koreme man who disappeared in this first sweep said he was taken away "because he was a man and not a child." Some of the boys who were taken had not been initially classed with the young and adult men, and were taken from their mothers. Many of those taken were teenagers.

All of the Koreme men who disappeared were taken away in the first sweep. A few others survived, in some cases perhaps because they were boys who looked very young for their age, and in some cases perhaps because they looked older than they were. The wounded survivor of the Koreme execution, Aba, was not taken. However, a day or so later, a second sweep was conducted, carrying away still more men and boys from other villages. By the conclusion of the sweeps, there were virtually no young adult men left among the captives in Dohuk.

The victims were loaded onto army trucks which left Dohuk fort. None of the Koreme men and boys who were taken away has ever been seen again.

Forced Relocation, and
the Dead Infant Girls of Jeznikam Cemetery

Beharke, Jeznikam, Qushtapa, Daratu, Binasirawa, Kasnazan, Sharways, Pirzin, Mala Omar, Segirtkan, Barhushtar, and Sebiran -- these are the names of some of the camps around the Kurdish city of Erbil to which tens of thousands of villagers from the surrounding mountains were forcibly relocated as part of the Anfal campaign.[1] Some, like Beharke, were large, with many thousands of inhabitants, and over time grew to merge with neighboring camps and eventually became collective towns. Others were small and remained discrete units.

Whatever their size, the camps lacked basic facilities and infrastructure, making it questionable whether they should be called "camps" at all. What does one call a flat, windswept plain, without buildings, without the systematic provision of food, water, sanitation, health care, blankets, huts, or shelters, onto which thousands of already weakened people were deposited over a few weeks at the beginning of autumn with winter approaching? The only structures were the guard towers with their machine guns, and the security buildings controlling the roads in and out. According to numerous accounts received by MEW/PHR, when asked by Kurdish villagers for food, water, and shelter, soldiers responded again and again, "Saddam has sent you here to die."

How Fakhir Survived in Salamia

Some of the surviving Kurdish villagers -- particularly elderly men -- went directly from regional forts like that in Dohuk to the camps. The old men of Koreme, after spending a few days in Dohuk fort, went directly by army truck to Beharke and Jeznikam, adjacent camps located about half an hour outside the Kurdish city of Erbil, and which together were the largest in the area.

Many of the women and children went from forts like Dohuk to still other forts. The women and children of Koreme were sent from Dohuk to a fort located near Salamia, a small town between Erbil and

---

[1] Some of these were also the names of towns or villages near the location of the camps.

61

Mosel. They stayed there two weeks before being moved to Beharke to join the older men.

Conditions were generally better in Salamia than Dohuk, as the villagers received more food. As at Dohuk, several thousand displaced people, almost all of them women and children, were crowded into the fort. The guards distributed a single piece of bread per person for the whole day, but also "chicken broth and sometimes rice and other staples," according to one woman who was there with three young children. There was a regular water supply. In addition, the guards let the detainees out of the fort to buy food at small shops in Salamia.

Still, there were risks at Salamia. Fakhir, a 15-year-old boy from Koreme, had originally been in the execution line-up at Koreme, but a soldier took him out, presumably because he looked too young. Fakhir was fortunate to look younger than his age, because other teenage boys his age perished at Koreme, and others disappeared in the fort at Dohuk. In Salamia, however, an officer, a first lieutenant, asked for his identification card. Fakhir's mother produced it, and when the officer saw his date of birth -- 1973 -- he said, "Why are you here? You're too old to be here." According to Fakhir, his mother tried to "tell the soldier I was too young, I was too small. She understood what they would have done with me. I didn't know. I thought they would take me to do hard labor until it was time to join the army. I didn't know."

The officer took Fakhir by the arm and walked him to the post at the main gate of the Salaman security fort. At the main gate, Fakhir said, was an old man who had not been taken directly to the camps with the others. The old man said, "Don't take this boy, do him a good deed, Saddam didn't say you had to take this one." The officer hesitated, and the old man continued, "Saddam won't see if you don't take him. Saddam's not watching. Do good in the sight of Allah, the compassionate, the merciful."

The officer let go of Fakhir, shook him roughly, and said, "Don't let me see you again. I was kind to you this once, but I won't be kind the next time." The old man told Fakhir to go hide with his mother "and stay out of sight. Don't let anyone see you."

Fakhir's two uncles, Zober Mostafa Saleh and Zahir Mostafa Saleh, had been executed at Koreme. His father, Taha Mostafa, had not been with the villagers when they were captured; according to Fakhir, "he had 10,000 Iraqi dinar and tried to bribe his way across the border. But they wouldn't let him across." Fakhir was told by other relatives that his father was captured by soldiers, wounded in the leg, and eventually brought to Dohuk fort after his family had been transferred south. Fakhir heard from others, but was unable to confirm, that his father had died of a beating in Dohuk fort; he thought he was buried in Dohuk cemetery, but could not be sure. The last time Fakhir saw his father alive was in the mountains on the way to the Turkish border, when the villagers turned back and Fakhir's father decided to try the border crossing alone.

The Generosity of the People of Erbil

After two weeks at Salamia, the women and children of Koreme, along with thousands of others, were taken and left at Beharke and Jeznikam. When they left Salamia, they asked the soldiers where they were being taken. According to Fakhir, the guards said, "There's been an amnesty. We're taking you back to your village."

But instead of taking them to the mountains, the soldiers took them instead to the plains outside the city of Erbil, a journey of four hours by road. The place consisted of barren fields, with a perimeter marked by guard towers and a security post at the main road. Those newly arrived spent hours searching for the old men of their village, who they hoped would be there, but could not know for sure.

In Beharke, there was nothing. There were no buildings, no shelters, no blankets against the cold at night, no protection from the sun during the day, no systematic provision of water or food, and no medical care. The administrators of Anfal appear not to have contemplated any need for these. The conclusion is unavoidable that they saw no reason to make any attempt, however minimal, to provide such amenities, because they were indifferent to whether these people lived or died.

All told the Iraqi military and Ba'th Party authorities mobilized hundreds of thousands of soldiers and militia and forcibly relocated hundreds of thousands of Kurds in a coordinated operation lasting many months. To refuse in the final phase of that operation to make any systematic provision, no matter how ineffectual, for elementary food and shelter for the relocated, makes it clear that official policy was that these people might as well die. Deliberately killing by malnutrition, disease, and exposure is as much murder as killing by firing squad.

The survival of the people in the camps around Erbil, including Beharke and Jeznikam, was due to the efforts of the fellow Kurds from Erbil. They organized a prodigious relief effort, bringing into the camps food, water, blankets, and later the materials necessary to build primitive shelters. Many people -- mostly children -- died in the camps, but the number would have been immeasurably greater but for the relief supplied from Erbil. One woman said, "They brought us food, clothes, vegetables and fruits, and later, what we needed to build our huts, everything. The army brought us nothing."

At the beginning, especially, the residents of Erbil ran personal risks entering Beharke clandestinely. The camp was not surrounded by barbed wire or fences, but only by guard towers; the women, children, and elderly located there had no means or anywhere to go. Erbil residents were not allowed official entrance to the camp and had to enter through the fields. Occasionally, in the first days, they were shot at. Other times they were picked up by soldiers and beaten, and sometimes taken in for questioning. After the first few days, however, the guards became more relaxed about allowing Erbil relief incursions, and by the end of a year essentially ignored them. But the most extraordinary feature of the Erbil relief effort was how long it went on as a voluntary endeavor; the city supported the people in the camps from the time they first arrived in September 1988 to the March 1991 Kurdish uprising, when most of the camp's residents were able to return home.

Still, the efforts of the people of Erbil could not prevent many deaths. Most of these deaths were among the infants and children, and they included Fakhir's baby sister, Farman Taha Mostafa. "My mother's milk," he said, "dried up in Dohuk after a few days." Under the better conditions in Salamia it returned, but failed again in Beharke. After two months in Beharke, in November 1988, Farman died, at the age of one year, of what cause exactly -- disease, general exposure, malnutrition, or dehydration -- no one knew. Fakhir took his sister's body, washed it and wrapped it as best he was able according to Islamic precept, and buried it in a shallow grave in the cemetery of Jeznikam. The cemetery had originally been that of an ancient village, but gradually was taken over by the dead from Beharke and Jeznikam camps, whose graves greatly expanded its perimeters.

Within a few months after the Kurdish villagers arrived at Beharke, epidemics spread through the camp. Kurdish doctors from Erbil, who clandestinely entered the camp in November and December 1988 and January 1989, found epidemics of typhoid, hepatitis, and cholera, in addition to more routine, but deadly, dysentery and influenza. "We tried to come into the camp with medicines at the front gate," said one Kurdish Erbil doctor, "but the soldiers wouldn't let us." But the soldiers let them sneak through the back roads. Indeed, several Kurdish

Erbil doctors expressed the view that the reason the Baghdad regime eventually tolerated unofficial but regular shipments of food and supplies from the Kurdish people of Erbil, and after a year set up an official medical post, was that it feared the spread of disease from the camps, in particular a possible cholera epidemic.

By the end of the first year, in late 1989, the government had relaxed its grip on the residents of the camps. They were issued identity cards, and allowed to spend the daytime working in Erbil. Those who could worked as day laborers; these were mostly old men and boys, since the young and adult men had largely been killed or had disappeared earlier. The camps gradually came to resemble the collective towns in which the government had relocated Kurds in earlier, pre-Anfal campaigns. By the end of 1990, the military authorities occasionally gave permission to some of the elderly men to make trips back to their village lands. The external political situation had shifted by then; the 1991 Gulf War was about to begin, and the regime's attention was apparently elsewhere. It was on one of these extended passes that the old man from Koreme returned to the village and put up a cinder block wall around the burial place of the executed men of Koreme, who included his own sons.

With the March 1991 uprising, the Iraqi army went south, most of the people of the camps were able to leave them for good and went back to the mountains. The people of Koreme returned to Dohuk city, and to Mengish; some went to Koreme, where they lived in tents and began rebuilding. A few, the poorest widows, with no extended family to help them and their young children, remained behind in Beharke camp.

The Graves of Three Infant Girls At Jeznikam Cemetery

The forensic team conducted investigations at Jeznikam cemetery between June 18 and 20, 1992. The purpose of the investigation was to determine whether archaeological evidence at the gravesites and evidence gathered from skeletal remains was consistent with the accounts given by Koreme villagers. The forensic team also proposed to exhume the skeleton of Fakhir's sister to determine what, if anything, could be said of the cause and manner of her death. The forensic team sought to determine if it could confirm basic elements of Fakhir's account of life in Beharke by finding the grave of his sister, Farman Taha Mostafa, where he indicated it was located and in the condition he said he had left it.

The site. Jeznikam cemetery is located on a small conical tell about 10 meters high and 135 meters across. It consists of (i) an older cemetery located atop the tell and associated with an older village that was reportedly destroyed by the Iraqi army in 1987, and (ii) a newer cemetery on the southern and eastern slopes of the tell containing -- according to Koreme villagers, current inhabitants of Jeznikam, and Erbil residents -- the graves of the dead of Jeznikam and Beharke camps. The portion of the cemetery comprising graves from the camp covers an area roughly 30 x 101 meters on the southern edge and 10 x 100 meters on the eastern edge.

JEZNIKAM
OLD CEMETERY

Transect 1	Transect 2	Transect 3	Transect 4	Transect 5	Transect 6	Transect 7
180 cm	220 cm	150 cm	160 cm	170 cm	none	none
150 cm	165 cm	245 cm	230 cm	250 cm		
130 cm	140 cm	250 cm	190 cm	190 cm		
210 cm	155 cm	150 cm	165 cm	140 cm		
200 cm	170 cm	205 cm	210 cm	100 cm		
170 cm	100 cm	200 cm	140 cm	130 cm		
110 cm	205 cm	170 cm	240 cm	200 cm		
70 cm	120 cm	160 cm	190 cm	205 cm		
180 cm	130 cm	260 cm	210 cm	90 cm		
90 cm	110 cm	160 cm	190 cm	145 cm		
185 cm	145 cm	170 cm	190 cm	260 cm		
160 cm	120 cm	130 cm		220 cm		
165 cm	165 cm	190 cm		200 cm		
80 cm	190 cm	170 cm		120 cm		
230 cm	150 cm	190 cm		190 cm		
170 cm	165 cm	190 cm				
150 cm	260 cm					
180 cm	155 cm					
180 cm	130 cm					
210 cm	120 cm					
190 cm	175 cm					
100 cm	190 cm					
180 cm	225 cm					
230 cm	170 cm					
230 cm						
70 cm						
140 cm						
245 cm						
210 cm						
210 cm						

JEZNIKAM
NEW CEMETERY

Transect 1	Transect 2	Transect 3	Transect 4	Transect 5	Transect 6	Transect 7
240 cm	200 cm	220 cm	67 cm	205 cm	110 cm	270 cm
100 cm	110 cm	210 cm	110 cm	135 cm	100 cm	90 cm
120 cm	100 cm	135 cm	245 cm	115 cm	90 cm	100 cm
140 cm	190 cm	160 cm	225 cm	235 cm	100 cm	110 cm
120 cm	125 cm	130 cm	240 cm	140 cm	100 cm	290 cm
130 cm	110 cm	120 cm	200 cm	160 cm	100 cm	235 cm
125 cm	120 cm	130 cm	240 cm	150 cm	95 cm	245 cm
135 cm	140 cm	130 cm	130 cm	150 cm	110 cm	240 cm
140 cm	120 cm	145 cm	155 cm	140 cm	110 cm	200 cm
135 cm	125 cm	100 cm		130 cm	140 cm	240 cm
120 cm	120 cm	135 cm		80 cm	110 cm	110 cm
120 cm	130 cm			130 cm	180 cm	120 cm
125 cm	170 cm			110 cm	210 cm	200 cm
145 cm				200 cm	160 cm	240 cm
210 cm					150 cm	165 cm
					140 cm	140 cm
						100 cm
						280 cm
						260 cm
						230 cm
						150 cm
						120 cm
						110 cm

The sample inventory of graves. The forensic team conducted a sample inventory of the graves in the cemetery to compare the ratio of adult and child graves in the old village versus the new detainee sectors of the cemetery.

For statistical purposes, a series of seven parallel transects was walked from south to north across the tell. Each grave intersecting with a transect was measured in centimeters from head to foot stone, and it was noted whether the grave was from the old village or new detainee portion of the cemetery. The transects covered approximately 20% of the total graves in the cemetery and in the opinion of the forensic team represent an accurate statistical sample of the cemetery.

A total of 166 graves fell within the sample. Taking into account the disappearance of many adult men prior to the arrivals of the detainees at the camp, it appears that a disproportionate number of deaths occurred among the children of detainees. The ratio of subadult to adult graves in the detainee sector is about five subadult graves for each adult grave. By contrast, the ratio of subadult to adult graves in the village sector of the cemetery, representing a "normal" distribution, is only about one subadult grave to two adult graves. It is evident that children suffered heavily in detention.[2]

The exhumation of Farwan Tawa Mostafa. The forensic team undertook the exhumation of three graves in the detainee sector of the cemetery. The purpose of these exhumations was to determine if they contained forensic evidence either consistent or inconsistent with detainee accounts of conditions of the camp. The three graves exhumed each contained the skeletal remains of an infant female. Two of the three showed signs of severe malnutrition and/or disease stress.

One of the three graves exhumed was that identified by Fakhir as that of his infant sister, Farwan Tawa Mostafa, who he said had died in the camp along with her mother, and both of whom he had buried with his own hands. The forensic team opened the grave identified by Fakhir as his sisters, and found the skeleton of an infant female, interred in the dress that Fakhir had described.

Forensic examination of the remains showed that she had been about seven months old, according to dentition, but only one to three months old, according to bone development. Fakhir reported her being

---

[2] See Appendix 1 for a complete discussion of the sample inventory of graves.

about one year. The difference in age determination between dentition and skelation is evidence of malnutrition and/or disease, because typically dentition develops normally while skeletal growth is severely retarded in the case of malnutrition or disease. The forensic team found this evidence supportive of detainee accounts of the privations suffered in the camp. It found no physical evidence that was inconsistent with survivor testimony.

Following the forensic examination, the remains of Farwan Tawa Mostofa and the other two infant females were reinterred according to Islamic precept.

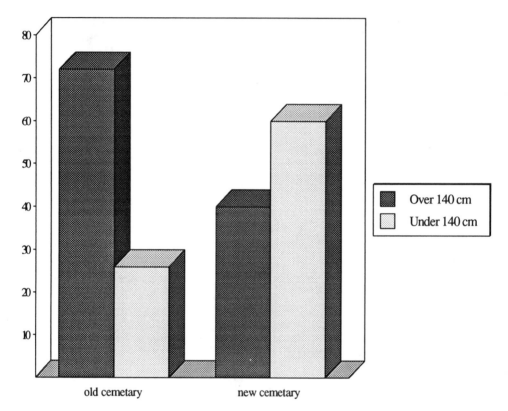

■	Over 140 cm	
□	Under 140 cm	

NUMBER OF GRAVES LARGER AND SMALLER THAN 140 cm
AT THE OLD AND NEW JEZNIKAM CEMETARIES.

The Destruction of Koreme

On August 29, 1988, Koreme was uninhabited. The bodies of those massacred lay where they had fallen, unburied, stiffened with rigor mortis, and starting to swell in the summer heat; according to Mengish residents, they were covered over with earth only several weeks later. Koreme's remaining villagers were in the hands of army forces in Mengish, and would soon be transferred to Dohuk. There the men would disappear, while the remainder would eventually make their way to Beharke and Jeznikam.

But the Anfal campaign was planned differently from earlier campaigns against the Kurds. One difference was that the Baghdad regime planned that the rural Kurds -- those rural Kurds, anyway, who remained alive -- would never return to their lands. In keeping with this strategic goal, the Anfal campaign devoted astonishing resources to the "destruction and removal of the remnants of the saboteurs and their premises."[1] In practice, this meant that the army destroyed whole villages down to the foundations of their buildings. Many of these buildings, the schools and often the mosques, had been built by the government only a few years before at some expense. Koreme was typical of the many destroyed villages seen by the forensic team in its travels through Iraqi Kurdistan.

Prior to Anfal, Koreme had some 160 houses made from mud bricks or from stone and cement; it also had a school and a mosque made from stone and cement. It had limited irrigation works attached to its springs. Electricity was installed in 1987. Following Anfal, nothing was left. The houses were gone. The school and mosque had been destroyed down to the foundations. The power lines were pulled down and the power poles knocked over. Between 1988 and 1992, vegetation had overgrown the site so that only the rubble of the school and mosque suggested to the uninitiated that there had once been a village there. Wildflowers that grow best in disturbed earth sprang up, and in the spring, much of the flattened village was covered with mustard flowers, dandelion, and Queen Anne's lace. The orchards had been burned, and the vineyards uprooted.

---

[1] "The End of Anfal" at 33.

The village springs were cemented over, and cement was poured into the wells.

Both the forensic team's archaeological examination of the destruction at Koreme and captured Iraqi army documents show that the destruction was neither the product of battle nor simply an afterthought. Instead it was a carefully planned, executed and integral part of Anfal. "The End of Anfal" notes that the "magnitude of the engineering work" needed to carry out the destruction of the villages "was so big that it put an extra burden on the shoulders of the command of a unit," particularly in the "procurement and distribution of explosives."[2]

Explosives indeed performed a sizable part of the Iraqi army's destructive work. The forensic team archaeologist noted the clean lines of debris in Koreme and other villages, including Birjinni. These lines are consistent with implosions, occasioned by explosives placed inside the buildings, causing them to collapse on themselves, without throwing debris outward. However, the success of such operations required the use of highly trained demolition squads, as "The End of Anfal" confirmed.

The forensic team archaelogist's conclusions are buttressed by the testimony of a Christian priest who witnessed the destruction of an Assyrian Christian church in April 1987 in the village of Bakhtoma. The priest said he was allowed to remain behind to collect certain items. He said he watched army demolition teams placing dynamite inside the church and other permanent structures in the village that could not be destroyed by bulldozer, and then watched the explosion.[3]

The villagers' possessions, particularly their animals and livestock, were plundered. One Kurdish man serving in the army at the time of Anfal reported seeing "huge pens where what they called 'the animals of the saboteurs'" were kept. Other Kurds in the Iraqi army at that time reported seeing "the animals of the saboteurs" being sold to Iraqi Arabs at cheap prices.

---

[2] "The End of Anfal" at 33.

[3] See note 8, chapter IV, The Chemical Weapons Attack on Birjinni, p. 41.

Conclusions of Fact and Law

MEW/PHR have reached the following principal conclusions concerning the foregoing events, based on the testimony the forensic team received and the physical forensic evidence it examined. In the view of MEW/PHR, these conclusions would be accepted by a court of law operating in conformity with internationally accepted standards of due process.

Conclusions of Fact

1.   Koreme and Birjinni are Kurdish villages in Dohuk governorate that were enveloped by Iraqi army forces during August 1988 in the course of the Anfal campaign.

2.   Anfal was an operation of the Iraqi government and army, occurring in part during August 1988, which had as its intent the depopulation of extensive zones of rural Kurdistan, the death or forced relocation of great numbers of Kurdish villagers, and the complete physical destruction of great numbers of Kurdish villages in those zones. Although the forensic team saw ample evidence of the depopulation of wide zones, death or forced relocation of great numbers of Kurdish villagers, and the complete destruction of great numbers of Kurdish villages, it was not in a position to offer more specific assessments of the extent of destruction across Iraqi Kurdistan. It leaves this matter to be determined by other MEW and PHR investigations.

3. The inhabitants of Koreme (including villagers from Chalkey) and Birjinni attempted to flee from the Iraqi army's Anfal operations on foot and by animal to Turkey during the last week of August 1988. Most were unsuccessful and returned to their villages, although some Birjinni villagers did finally reach Turkey.

4. Anfal operations conducted by the Iraqi army included the chemical weapons bombardment of Birjinni on or about August 25, 1988. Four Birjinni villagers died as a result of this attack, and an undetermined number were injured.

5.   Eyewitness descriptions of symptoms experienced from chemical weapons injuries are consistent with those received by PHR in

73

investigations it conducted in Turkey of similar bombardments.[1] Descriptions of symptoms by victims and eyewitnesses are tentatively consistent with the use of nerve agents.

6. On August 28, 1988, Koreme villagers (including villagers from Chalkey), numbering between 150 and 300 men, women, and children, together with their animals, returned from an unsuccessful flight to Turkey, surrendering to an Iraqi army unit at the outskirts of Koreme village.

7. On the afternoon of August 28, 1988, two Iraqi army lieutenants in charge of the Iraqi army unit ordered a group of men and boys from Koreme to form a line and squat. They reduced the line to thirty three men and boys by removing some (apparently young boys) from the line and sending them to join their families, who were taken to a place near the village school, out of sight, but not out of earshot, of the line of men and boys.

8. One of the Iraqi army officers communicated with his headquarters in Mengish by walkie-talkie, asking for instructions on what to do with the prisoners in the line. Although there were no witnesses to the reply sent by walkie-talkie, he was apparently instructed to execute the prisoners. Evidence from other locations, e.g. the village of Mergatou, shows a similar pattern of executions on orders from local headquarters.

9. Immediately upon receiving a reply from headquarters in Mengish, the officer ordered the soldiers guarding the line of Koreme men and boys -- approximately fifteen soldiers armed with automatic rifles -- to open fire. At least seven soldiers did so, one approaching the victim line and having to reload at least once. Following several volleys of fire, several soldiers were ordered to approach the fallen men and boys, and they delivered additional shots as coups de grace into the mass of bodies.

10. Of the thirty three men and boys in the line, twenty seven died. Six survived the execution, one of whom later disappeared after being seized again by Iraqi forces.

11. The dead men and boys were left unburied for some time, and were eventually deposited in two mass graves near where they fell by

---

[1] See generally *Winds of Death*.

74

Iraqi soldiers. The graves were undisturbed from the time of burial to the time of exhumation by the forensic team.[2]

12. Surviving Koreme villagers were removed by Iraqi army forces to detention first at Mengish and later at Dohuk. Conditions in detention included very little food or water during the three to five days most villagers were held there.

13. While in detention at Dohuk fort, on or about September 1, 1988, approximately twenty six Koreme men and boys, comprising nearly all the remaining adult and teenage males of Koreme village, disappeared at the hands of Iraqi security forces. Men and boys from many other villages who were also detained in the fort also disappeared.

14. The removal of the approximately twenty six Koreme men and boys was carried out by guards and other Iraqi army or security agents at Dohuk, and MEW/PHR consider their fate to be the responsibility of the Iraqi government. The evidence suggests that the disappeared men are dead, and that they were killed by Iraqi forces.

15. Surviving elderly men of Koreme were taken from Dohuk fort to the camps of Beharke and Jeznikam, near Erbil.

16. Surviving women and children of Koreme were taken from Dohuk fort to a facility at Salamia, where they remained approximately two weeks. Food was distributed on a regular basis at Salamia fort.

17. After approximately two weeks at Salamia fort, surviving women and children of Koreme were removed to the camps of Beharke and Jeznikam.

18. These camps consisted of a perimeter of guard towers and a security post at the main entrance. The camps contained no shelters or structures for the relocated. During the first two to three months, until approximately December 1988, Iraqi authorities made no systematic provision for food, water, blankets, medicine, or medical care for the people they had forcibly relocated there. The people slept in the open during the first several months.

19. Supplies on which the Koreme villagers and other relocated persons survived were not provided by Iraqi authorities, but on a voluntary basis by residents of the nearby Kurdish city of Erbil. Iraqi authorities initially opposed such voluntary aid, and so supplies had to be brought clandestinely and at great risk into the camp. Iraqi authorities

---

[2] Dr. Snow made an exploratory entry into the graves in March 1992 prior to the arrival of the full forensic team in May 1992.

gradually relaxed the prohibition on supplies. Several months after the arrival of the forcibly relocated in Beharke, the Iraqi government began making some shipments of supplies, and at the end of the first year, in approximately September 1989, it established a medical post in Beharke.

20. Many persons, especially infants and children, died at Beharke and Jeznikam from causes resulting directly from the Iraqi policy of not supplying basic necessities to those it had forcibly relocated. Causes of death included exposure, malnutrition, dehydration, and disease. Epidemics of serious diseases, including typhoid and cholera, took place in the camps by reason of the policy of the Iraqi government of refusing even minimally to provide for the survival of those it had taken into custody. Infants and children appear to have constituted approximately two-thirds of the total deaths suffered in Beharke and Jeznikam camps, on the basis of the survey of graves at Jeznikam cemetery.

21. The forensic team found physical evidence of malnutrition in the skeletal remains of Farman Taha Mostafa, a female infant who was born in Koreme and died in Beharke-Jeznikam at the age of approximately one year. On the basis of physical evidence it was not possible to determine whether she died of malnutrition, disease or some other cause, although there was no evidence of trauma to the skeleton.

22. The refusal to provide minimal conditions for the maintenance of life to those forcibly relocated to the camps appears to have been an official policy of the Iraqi government, and not due to administrative confusion, errors, or negligence. Based on (i) the Iraqi government's refusal to provide the minimal conditions to maintain life, (ii) repeated statements by soldiers to forcibly relocated persons that they had been sent to the camps to die, (iii) the logistical sophistication of other phases of the Anfal campaign, (iv) the general aims of the Anfal campaign as demonstrated in the use of chemical weapons against unarmed civilians, mass executions, and mass disappearances, and (v) captured Iraqi army documents, MEW/PHR conclude that the Iraqi government intended the deaths of many, if not all, of those forcibly relocated to the camps.

23. The Iraqi government appears to have intended that exposure, malnutrition, and disease in the camps would accomplish what would otherwise require setting up an active machinery of killing. The Iraqi government appears to have carried out this homicidal intention during the first two to three months after the forcibly relocated arrived at the camps; in subsequent months it appears to have relaxed its

vigilance. It finally gave up this aim by the end of the first year, lapsing into mere negligence.

24. In the spring of 1991, by reason of the 1991 Gulf War and the March 1991 Kurdish uprising, Koreme survivors were able to leave Beharke and Jeznikam and return to Koreme.

25. The physical premises of Koreme, including approximately 160 houses, a school, a mosque, electric power lines, and irrigation facilities, were totally destroyed down to the foundations by the Iraqi army, using trained demolition squads. This destruction was not collateral damage in the course of army operations, either legitimate or illegitimate, but part of a specific Iraqi government policy to destroy Kurdish villages, and an integral part of the Anfal campaign.

Conclusions of Law

1. The executions and disappearances of Koreme men and boys, the forcible relocation of surviving villagers, the conditions in detention centers and the relocation camps resulting in the death and severe suffering of surviving villagers, and the destruction of Koreme's physical premises, and the chemical attacks on and destruction of the village of Birjinni, if shown to be undertaken with "intent to destroy, in whole or in part, a national, ethnical, racial, or religious group," constitute genocidal acts by the government of Iraq and by the individuals who ordered or carried them out.[3]

2. The executions and disappearances of Koreme men and boys, the forcible relocation of surviving villagers, the conditions in detention and the camps resulting in deaths and severe suffering among surviving villagers, and the destruction of Koreme's physical premises, as well as the chemical attacks on and destruction of the village of Birjinni, constitute "crimes against humanity," within the meaning of that term as used in the 1945 Nuremberg Tribunal, by the government of Iraq and by the individuals who ordered or carried them out.[4]

---

[3] See the Genocide Convention, reproduced at Appendix 4.

[4] See Appendix 5 for a memorandum stating Human Rights Watch's view of the legal elements for "crimes against humanity" applied to events described in this report.

77

3. The executions and resulting deaths of twenty seven Koreme men and boys were murder by the Iraqi government and by army forces who ordered or carried them out.

4. The disappearances and presumed deaths of approximately additional twenty six Koreme men and boys were murder by the Iraqi government and by army forces who ordered or carried them out.

5. The deaths of four Birjinni villagers in the chemical weapons attack in the last week of August 1988 were murder by the Iraqi government and by army forces who ordered or carried it out.

6. The death of Farman Taha Mostafa at Beharke camp in late 1988 was murder by the Iraqi government and by army forces who ordered or carried out actions implementing the intent to deny the minimal conditions for the maintenance of human life to those forcibly displaced and held in the camps.

7. The crimes and violations of human rights described in the foregoing are gross abuses of human rights by the government of Iraq within the meaning of United States laws governing, among other things, the provision of certain types of foreign assistance furnished to Iraq during the period following the aforementioned crimes at, inter alia, Koreme, Birjinni, Mengish, Dohuk, Beharke and Jeznikam in the course of the Anfal campaign up to the Iraqi invasion of Kuwait on August 2, 1990.[5] The extent of U.S. government knowledge of these crimes when they were taking place remains to determined.

8. The use of chemical weapons against Iraqi civilians is, in the opinion of HRW, a violation of customary international law by the government of Iraq.[6]

---

[5] See, inter alia, 22 U.S.C. section 2304 (1988) (Section 502B, Foreign Assistance Act of 1961, as amended); 22 U.S.C. section 2151n (1988) (Section 116 of the Foreign Assistance Act of 1961, as amended); and 7 U.S.C. section 1712 (1988) (Section 112 of the Agricultural Trade Development and Assistance Act of 1954, as amended).

[6] See generally Letter of Human Rights Watch to Rolf Ekeus, Chairman of the U.N. Special Commission on Iraq, dated December 30, 1992 for discussion of this customary law prohibition.

The Prayer Over the Dead at Koreme

"In the Name of God
The Compassionate
The Merciful

Praise be to God, Lord of the Universe,
The Compassionate, the Merciful,
Sovereign of the Day of Judgment!
You alone we worship, and to You alone
we turn for help.
Guide us to the straight path,
The path of those whom You have favored,
Not of those who have incurred Your wrath,
Nor of those who have gone astray."[1]

The mullah, the Muslim holy man, finished reciting The Exordium, the opening chapter of the Koran. The assembled men, standing at the head of the great trench opened by the bulldozer, recited the ritual responses, their palms turned upward to heaven. He continued with the prayer over the dead, customary with Sunni Muslims of Iraqi Kurdistan, consisting of instructions to those who died.[2]

"Oh servant of God, do not forget your covenant: that there is no God but He, and Muhammad is his prophet.

You have left this world and gone to the Hereafter, either to the Gardens of Paradise or to the hell of fire.

Now two Angels will come to you and ask:
Who is your God?
Who is your prophet?
What is your Qibla?

---

[1] *The Koran*, 1:1, trans. N.J. Dawood, Viking Press, 1990.

[2] Translated by a local Iraqi Kurd working with the forensic team, for whose help the forensic team is indebted.

Who are your brothers?
Who are your sisters?

You must answer clearly:
Allah is my God.
Muhammad is my prophet.
Mecca is my Qibla.
The Holy Koran is my guide.
Believing men are my brothers.
Believing women are my sisters."

Then the mullah took a handful of earth and, scattering it into the open trench, said:

"From this you were created, to it we return you now, and from it you will be brought forth again."

The men formed a line, passing from one to another the twenty seven individual wooden boxes containing the bones of Koreme's dead. The boxes were small and cubical, because they did not have to accommodate the skeleton laid out at full length. They had been built originally for the forensic team's use, to transport the skeletons from the mass grave site at Koreme to the morgue at Dohuk General Hospital. At the morgue, the skeletons had been painstakingly reassembled through weeks of work.

The forensic team had succeeded in positively identifying each of the twenty seven skeletons. After recording the facts of pathology and trauma bearing on cause and manner of death, it turned each skeleton and its effects over to the deceased's family. The families and the village decided on a joint funeral in conjunction with the local peshmerga and political party organization, in which the dead would be reburied according to proper Islamic rites in a new village cemetery.

On June 19, 1992, in the morning, the procession began from Dohuk morgue, a line of cars and trucks and Toyota Landcruisers that had been captured from the Iraqi security forces. Each box of remains was strapped to the top of a car, with flowers and often a photograph of the deceased; relatives rode inside, usually widows or mothers. Several hundred peshmerga fighters were also there carrying their weapons and wearing uniforms combining military dress and traditional Kurdish clothing. The line of cars slowly made its way out of Dohuk, passed through Mengish, and finally climbed the hill to Koreme. From the top of the hill, the mountain crest marking the border with Turkey, across which the dead men and their families had sought to flee, was visible in the distance; there were still snow patches on the peaks even though it was late June.

At the gravesite, there was no further need for the wooden boxes; in accordance with Islamic custom, the bones were to be buried wrapped in white linen. Inside the large grave trench, individual tombs had been laid of cement block; each linen sack of bones was laid in its tomb, the head facing toward Mecca. The top of each tomb was sealed with more cement blocks, and bunches of dry grass were laid on thickly. Men with shovels filled in earth around the individual tombs, and finally the bulldozer closed the trench.

The women did not join the men at the gravesite. They remained on the other side of the hill, mourning their dead with wailing and keening. A few young boys proudly carried their fathers' weapons slung across their shoulders through the crowd of mourners, assault rifles sometimes as tall as they were.

The forensic team's scientific leader, Dr. Clyde Collins Snow, gave an interview to local Kurdish television; it was a mistake, he said, for those who violated human rights to think they could hide their crimes by burying them. Ample evidence -- the evidence of the bones -- often remained.

There were political speeches by leaders of the local branch of the KDP. They eulogized the dead men and boys of Koreme as martyrs. They called them heroes and warriors of the Kurdish struggle, whereas in fact they were frightened and desperate men seeking refuge for themselves and their families. But, in the midst of Anfal there was no refuge to be found. And the teenage boys who died were just boys who, on a day in late August 1988, were lined up on the slope of a hill outside their own village and shot.

The disappeared of Koreme remained disappeared. After the funeral the forensic team's engineer, a Kurdish man of great devoutness, remembered them aloud. He expressed the hope that the skulls of the disappeared, whether buried under the sands of some Iraqi desert, or in a shallow grave in the courtyard of a fortress, or somewhere else, were facing toward Mecca and that they would not be forgotten.

Thus Koreme's dead were laid away.

APPENDICES

1. Archaeological Report on Koreme, Birjinni, and Jeznikam - Beharke Cemetery

2. Forensic Anthropology Report

3. Report on Firearms Identification at the Koreme Execution Site

4. Convention on the Prevention and Punishment of the Crime of Genocide

5. Memorandum: The Elements of Crimes Against Humanity Applied to The Destruction of Koreme

---

Acknowledgments

Maps

Plans and Diagrams

Photographs

APPENDIX 1

Archaeological Report on
Koreme, Birjinni, and Jeznikam-Beharke Cemetery

by
James Briscoe,
Forensic Team Archaeologist[1]

and

Clyde Collins Snow,
Forensic Team Scientific Leader[2]

Introduction

Archaeological investigations were carried out at three sites in Kurdistan, Northern Iraq, between May 25 and June 24, 1992 as part of investigations by Middle East Watch and Physicians for Human Rights ("MEW/PHR") into allegations of gross violations of human rights possibly amounting to genocide by the government of Iraq against Iraqi Kurds during the Anfal campaign of 1988. Archaeological expertise was considered an important part of these investigations in order to provide a precise record of events and remains at the sites investigated. These investigations were part of a multidisciplinary approach including forensic anthropology, oral history, ballistic analysis, and review of written documentation.

Archaeological investigations between May 25 and June 24, 1992 were limited to three sites, with the major emphasis on the village of Koreme, district of Mengish, Dohuk governorate, Iraqi Kurdistan, and a mass grave site at Koreme initially explored by Dr. Snow, forensic

---

[1] Mr. Briscoe is a field archaeologist with Roberts/ Schornik & Associates, Inc., Norman, Oklahoma, to whom MEW/PHR express thanks for making Mr. Briscoe available for the extended length of the dig in Iraqi Kurdistan.

[2] Professor of Anthropology, University of Oklahoma, Norman, Oklahoma.

anthropologist and forensic team scientific leader, in February 1992. The second site was the village of Birjinni, district of Zawita, Dohuk governorate, Iraqi Kurdistan, selected because it was alleged to have been attacked with chemical weapons by the Iraqi army in August 1988. The third site was a cemetery at the Jeznikam-Beharke camp, near the city of Erbil, Erbil governorate, Iraqi Kurdistan, said to contain the remains of Kurds who died in the course of forcible relocations during the Anfal campaign of 1988.

Archaeological investigations included the general survey of the sites, mapping of salient features, controlled collection of artifacts and soil samples, and excavation of grave sites for forensic study.

This discussion incorporates by reference materials contained in the foregoing report, "The Destruction of Koreme During the Anfal Campaign."

Koreme

The village of Koreme is located in a small valley of the frontal range of the Zagros mountains about four kilometers north of the district capital of Mengish in Dohuk governorate.

The Village Site

Koreme, prior to its destruction, consisted of two clusters of buildings divided by a small stream running north-south through the center of the village. The prominent landmark of the village is a 10 meter hill used as the original village cemetery. There were originally about 100 houses in the village, including 50 belonging to members of the Barwari tribe to the west of the stream and 40 to 50 belonging to members of the Shearali tribe to the east of the stream.

Houses in the village were generally about 5 x 8 meters in plan, with a few larger structures interspersed throughout the village. The average house was made of mud bricks, while the larger structures were made primarily from concrete blocks with limestone stem walls averaging about 30 cm.

The village school was located on the southeast edge of the village and was used as a reference point for mapping the village. (See Koreme Village Plan.) The school was a 15 x 20 meter two room building made of limestone and reinforced concrete. The village mosque was located on the northwestern edge of the village and appeared similar to the school in size and design.

Koreme was bordered on the north, east, and west by agricultural lands, which in May and June 1992 were mostly fallow. Smaller garden plots were reopened in 1991-92 throughout the village, and one larger field was in cultivation about 800 meters west of the village. Forensic team investigators were shown a U.S.-made star shell on the south side of the field, rigged with a trip wire to one end; it is not known whether or not it was an operational booby trap, although local informants commented on problems with landmines in the fields. There is a large orchard on the south side of village and several smaller vineyards scattered about the area.

At the time of the forensic team's investigations in May and June 1992, all village structures, including houses, the school, and the mosque, had been destroyed down to the foundations. The mud houses appeared to have been bulldozed and, in some cases, possibly dynamited. The concrete and limestone structures appeared to have been dynamited.

The pattern of rubble scatter was significant in that it was primarily inside the structures and following neat lines, indicating interior charge placement with some care and expertise in demolition. Demolition appears to have been systematic, and there appears to have been no battle or other fighting resulting in artillery or bombardment damage to the structures. So far as could be determined, the destruction of Koreme was carried out by demolition and bulldozer, in a systematic fashion. The rubble of the village school contained a visible trip wire sticking out of the concrete remains, which local informants said was connected to a mine or booby trap.

The execution and grave sites are located across a small hill on the west side of the village, about 200 meters from the village proper.

The Execution Site

The execution site consists of the two lines along which, according to oral testimony and forensic evidence, the Iraqi firing squad stood and the Koreme victims squatted. (See Plan of Execution Site.) The execution site is on the steeper west slope of the hill and not directly visible from the village proper. A fallow plowed field in 1992 extends from the top of the hill to the upper edge of the execution site. According to local informants, this field was first plowed following the 1988 execution in 1991 and the edge of the execution site may have been

87

impacted somewhat. The majority of the execution site, however, is located on a steeper slope that has not been plowed since the execution. The firing squad, according to oral testimony and ballistic analysis, stood along a line uphill from the line where the Koreme men squatted. Slope grade is 10% between the two lines, which are about 12 meters apart. The Koreme victims' line is located about 8.7 meters southeast of the south edge of the grave site.

The execution site was divided into two sections for controlled collection purposes. A metric grid was established along the firing line and artifacts were collected in meter strips along the baseline. Each cartridge brass was plotted according to its position along the baseline and given a numerical designation before collecting. The numerical designation was plotted on graph paper and written on the artifact as each was located and collected. A second grid line, keyed to the firing line baseline, was set up along the victims line for collection of artifacts there. All materials located between the two lines and outside the grid were measured in relation to the grid baseline.

Artifacts were collected by two forensic team archaeologists searching meter wide strips on hands and knees. Koreme villagers assisted by cutting grass and weeds from each strip as it was searched and by marking the locations of artifacts as they observed them. Special care was taken not to move any artifacts until they were plotted and numbered.

Several artifacts were found besides spent brass. A shrapnel fragment was found on the firing line. A lighter, comb, tin cup, and a pair of man's shoes were found on the victims' line. Two unfired rounds were found between the two grids and two misfired rounds were found on the firing line.

Spent brass and all records of location and plotting were sent for ballistic analysis, results of which are found in Appendix 3.

The Grave Site

The primary focus of forensic team investigations was the mass grave site, dating, according to oral testimony, from the execution during the 1988 Anfal campaign. The grave site consisted of two low (approximately .75 meter high) concrete brick enclosures, each 5 x 8 meters in size, located about 2 meters apart on a slope west of the village.

The two low-walled areas were designated Graves A and B for control purposes and the two pits in each grave were designated Grave

A-North, Grave A-South, Grave B-North, and Grave B-South so that each could be excavated separately. Bodies were given sequential numerical designations as they were exposed in each pit. (See Koreme Graves Plan.)

Each enclosure contained two roughly 2 x 2 meter pits. One pit, designated Grave B-S, contained several disturbances that appeared to be artillery shell craters predating the graves. Grave B-N included two similar disturbances and Grave A-S contained one. The four pits run along a line on the slope about 10 meters northwest of the line where the Koreme victims were killed. The site of the graves appears to have been based partly on the presence of existing holes, the shell craters. Shrapnel fragments were recovered from the shell crater disturbances. The grave site walls were made from 20 cm long concrete bricks.

Prior to actual excavation, the area within the two brick walls was cleared of brush and ground cover. The walls were then dismantled after mapping, to afford easier access to the graves and prevent collapse during excavation. the area around the grave site was also mapped, including the lines where the firing squad and Koreme victims had been.

The test made by Dr. Snow in February 1992 was reopened and expanded to cover the entire pit. Shovels were used to remove disturbed surface soils from the remainder of the grave pits before excavation commenced.

A "floating" grid system was established for each pit due to the habit of Koreme villagers of crowding around the excavations. Landmarks in each pit (pit outlines, skulls, other bones, etc.) were graphed for each of the drawings made and superimposed on a composite drawing in the laboratory. Photographs of each pit, landmarks, and body were periodically made for documentation and as a reference check for the composite map.

In the pits, excavation tools were confined to trowels, brushes, and bamboo picks. Standard professional procedures for excavating burials were followed at all times. Once remains were exhumation, the forensic team removed them following the system established by Dr. Snow in exhumations in Argentina. Artifacts, clothing, and skeletal remains were recorded on standard field inventory forms and removed from the grave pit in anatomical order (generally from foot to head in order). Evidence of trauma was noted on a skeletal checklist form as each bone was removed. All items were catalogued and bagged according to the numerical and pit designations assigned by the archaeologist in the field. This information was transferred to Case File numbers assigned to each body as it was received in the morgue in the nearby city of Dohuk.

Grave A. Grave A was a walled enclosure measuring 4.5 x 8 meters, roughly the same size and shape as most of the houses in Koreme village. The grave contained two burial pits designated Grave A-N and Grave A-S. The grave was erected on a gentle slope, running northeast downhill to southwest and is oriented on its long axis 40 degrees west of magnetic north. Slope in the walled grave is 8 per cent northeast to southwest.

Grave A-N is a shallow 1.7 x 2.7 meter pit in the north corner of the walled grave. Two bodies were located between 0.3 and 0.5 meters below the surface on one side of the pit. A conical disturbance, 60 cm across, was located in the northeast corner of the pit and is believed to have been an artillery shell crater, as suggested by shrapnel found in other similar disturbances.

Grave A-S is a larger and deeper pit, 2.8 x 3.2 meters, located in the southeast corner of the walled grave. The pit has an irregular outline and appears to have been expanded on one side prior to filling. Eight bodies were recovered from the eastern two-thirds of the pit below 0.4 to 0.8 meters of fill. The southwestern one-third of the pit contained 0.1 to 0.2 meters of fill and may have been too shallow for covering bodies.

Grave B. Grave B is located just southeast of Grave A and in a 5.2 x 9.1 meter enclosure oriented on its long axis 20 degrees west of magnetic north. The southwest corner of the wall is roughly 10 meters northwest of the line where the Koreme victims were squatting during the execution. Slope within the walled grave runs downhill east to west and is 5 per cent. There is a small almond tree in the center of the south half of the enclosure, planted by one of the local villagers in 1985, that served as the datum point for the grave site. Grave B also contained two burial pits, designated Grave B-N and Grave B-S.

Grave B-N is a 2.8 x 3 meter pit located in the northeast corner of the enclosure. Eight bodies were located in the pit between 0.1 and 0.35 meters deep. Two roughly 60 cm wide disturbances were noted on the east edge of the pit that contained a powdery white substance and shrapnel fragments and are believed to be artillery shell craters that existed prior to the grave pit. Bodies in the pit appeared to be more tightly packed and commingled than in the Grave A pits.

Grave B-S was located in the southeast corner of the enclosure and measured 1.9 x 2.35 meters. Nine bodies, tightly commingled, were found between 0.2 and 0.4 meters deep. Three roughly circular conical disturbances, 60 cm across, were found on the edges of the pit and are thought to be artillery shell craters predating the burial. At least four other similar disturbances were also noted within the Grave B enclosure but were not examined. One disarticulated humerus was found in the 0.2 meters of fill above the bodies.

Birjinni

The purpose of the visit to the village of Birjinni, district of Zawita, Dohuk governorate, on June 10, 1992, was to obtain data concerning chemical weapons attacks occurring in late August 1988.

The Birjinni Site

The village of Birjinni occupies a narrow saddle and mountain pass along a chain of higher ridges between the towns of Zakho and Dohuk. It comprises a tell 10 meters high and 100 meters wide. There is a low sloping terrace on the north side of the village, consisting of about 0.3 hectares with orchards and limited farmland. (See Plan of Birjinni Village.)

Birjinni had about 40 houses at the time of the attack in August 1988, some of stone and others of mud brick. It also had a school and mosque, each a two room building made from cement and stone. There were remains of two roads to the village, one leading to Dohuk and the other to Zawita. At the time of the June 1992 investigations, only the Zawita road was passable, and there were posted landmine warnings adjacent to the road. In June 1992, no buildings remained standing in Birjinni. The sites of the mosque, school, and houses had been destroyed down to the foundations, in the same fashion as that described in Koreme.

The Chemical Weapons Bomb Craters

Four bomb craters along the west edge of the terrace, about 700 meters from the village, were examined in detail. Visual confirmation of the locations of the other eight craters was also made.

The four craters examined in detail consisted of low conical depressions 2.2 meters across and 0.6 to 1.2 meters deep. Fragments of the bombs were found lying immediately beside and in the craters, and

91

in two instances consisted of an iron outer envelope, an aluminum inner canister, a heavy lid labelled "Top" in English, a spout in the lid, and twisted tail fins. The fragments near each crater in those two instances were sizable, approximately 1 meter by 0.5 meter by 0.5 meter, and approximately 10 kilos in weight. Small bits of a yellowish ocher-like substance were noted in the craters and scraped from inside a canister and, along with soil samples, have been sent for laboratory testing. The four craters were evenly spaced on a straight line thirty meters apart and may have been dropped from low altitude, on a line consistent with survivor reports of aircraft direction.

The Exhumation Site

The forensic team carried out exhumations of two reported chemical weapons victims buried on adjacent plots on the sloping terrace lying north of the village, down valley and near a stream flowing down from the saddle. The site of the exhumations was a wooded canyon, filled with both cultivated fruit and wild trees. The skeletal remains were removed from graves each approximately one meter deep. Standard procedures for exhumation and examination were followed, and the results noted in Dr. Snow's anthropological report. The two skeletons were reburied in the village cemetery following forensic examination in accordance with Islamic ritual.

Jeznikam-Beharke Cemetery

Jeznikam-Beharke cemetery, reported to contain the remains of forcibly relocated Kurds who had died after being brought to these camps outside Erbil, was examined between June 18 and 20, 1992. Archaeological investigations included a sample inventory of the camp graves compared to graves in the previously existing cemetery that had served the old village prior to establishment of the 1988 camps. Forensic examinations of three children's graves in the camp portion of the cemetery were carried out by Dr. Snow on site. The remains were replaced in their crypts once investigations were complete.

The Site

Jeznikam-Beharke cemetery is located on a small conical tell about ten meters high and 135 meters across. An older existing cemetery is located atop the tell and is associated with a nearby village that was destroyed by the Iraqi army in 1987 in the course of establishing the Jeznikam-Beharke camp.

The dead of Jeznikam-Beharke camp were reported by camp survivors to be buried on the southern and eastern slopes of the cemetery. The camp portion of the cemetery covers an area roughly 30 x 101 meters on the southern edge and 10 x 100 meters on the eastern edge.

Sample Inventory of Graves

Methodology. The forensic team's analysis accepted the proposition that, in populations under extreme stress, there would be not only an increase in overall mortality but also a shift toward a proportionally higher death rate among children. It also seemed reasonable to assume that the graves in the village part of the cemetery represented a fair picture of the long term mortality profile of Jeznikam village which, prior to Anfal, was a typical Kurdish community of its size. In such a community, we would expect the ratio of child to adult deaths, taken over many years, to be more or less constant. This ratio would be reflected in the proportion of child to adult burials in the village cemetery. It could therefore serve as a "control" with which to compare the corresponding ratio of the detainee section of the cemetery.

Kurdish burial custom requires that the dead be stripped of all clothing and adornments, washed, and wrapped in a plain linen shroud. Graves are normally dug to a depth of about 1.8 meters. The bottom, lower sides and ends of the grave are loosely lined with flat stones to form a crude coffin-like crypt. The fully-extended corpse is placed in the crypt with its head at the west end of the grave and lying on its left side so that it faces southward toward Mecca. After the body is properly positioned, the crypt is sealed with another layer of flat stones placed over the corpse and the grave is filled.

With few exceptions, the graves of Jeznikam offer no information on the identity of the dead. Following their tradition of extremely simple burial, Kurds do not ordinarily inscribe gravestones with the decedent's name, age, or date of death. However, because a grave is dug no longer than necessary comfortably to accommodate the corpse, its length is roughly proportional to that of the body. Stated more simply, the graves of children are shorter than those of adults. It follows that, within a given series of burials, the ratio of shorter to longer graves should provide an approximation of child mortality relative to that of adults. Therefore, the forensic team decided to use grave length as an index by which to compare the child mortality profile of the Jeznikam villagers during normal times with that of the detainees during their confinement in Jeznikam-Beharke camp.

A complete census of graves in the two sections could not be undertaken in the brief time available. Instead, the forensic team conducted a sampling survey based on a series of seven equally-spaced transects. Each transect spanned the entire breadth of the cemetery from north to south and thus included areas of both the village and detainee sectors. They were also perpendicular to the axes of the graves which are oriented from east to west. If a transect line passed between the head and foot stone of a grave, it was included in the sample and its length and sector recorded.

"Grave length" was defined as the distance to the nearest .05 meters between the top centers of the head and foot stones. It is somewhat longer than the actual length of the corpse, on account of the fact that the crypts are constructed to allow some free space between end walls and the corpse, and further because of the thickness of the stones forming the ends of the crypt. Based on previous observations of Kurdish burials, this difference appears to average about 30 cm. Accordingly, this amount was subtracted from measured length to obtain a truer approximation of "body length," which was to be used as the principal variable in our data analysis.

Since the purpose was to compare the proportion of children's graves to those of adults, it was necessary to develop a reasonable criterion for distinguishing them based on estimates of body length. To do so, the forensic team utilized Field's anthropometric survey of Iraqi Kurds.[3] From Field's data -- the most extensive to date -- it appears that a range between 141 cm (female mean - 2SD) and 178 cm (male mean + 2SD) would embrace about 96.5% of Kurdish adults of both sexes. Based on this, the forensic team classified burials shorter than 141 cm. as "subadult" and those 141 and longer as "adult." There would inevitably

---

[3] Field, *The Anthropology of Iraq*, Harvard (1952).

be some overlap on account of exceptionally short adults or larger adolescents; these two categories would tend to offset each other.

    Results. A total of 166 graves fell within the sampling parameters. Of these, 81 (48.8% were in the village sector and the remaining 85 (51.2%) were in the detainee sector. In the village sector, subadult burials comprise 45 of the total of 81 sampled burials or by a ratio of 1.25. Such a finding is not unexpected in a peasant society where childhood mortality from epidemic disease is high and health care not good. In contrast, subadults in the detainee sector comprise 71 (83.5%) of the sample 85 burials. In the detainee sector, the subadult to adult ratio is 5.07. A Chi-square analysis of the distribution shows that the difference between the two sectors is statistically significant at the .0001 probability level.

    However, the very high subadult to adult ratio of graves in the detainee sector cannot be attributed entirely to a higher mortality rate among children. A second factor influencing the ratio relates to the Iraqi government's elimination of substantial numbers of adult males either by execution or forcible disappearance prior to the transfer of remaining detainees to the camp. For this reason, the adult component of the detainee population had already been reduced by the time the detainees had reached Jeznikam. This fact has the effect of making the subadult to adult grave ratio in the detainee sector less statistically unusual. To assess this effect, the forensic team calculated the distribution of subadult and adult graves that would be expected if two-thirds of the males had been eliminated from the detainee population prior to the detainees' arrival at Jeznikam. When this hypothetical distribution is compared to that actually observed in the detainee sector the difference is still significant at the .05 probability level.

    Thus, it is evident that a disproportionate number of deaths occurred among children of the detainees, as substantiated by the ratio of subadult to adult graves in the detainee sector of the cemetery. This ratio, which amounts to about five subadult graves to one adult grave, is significantly higher than that observed in the village sector, which was taken as representative of the normal mortality profile among rural Kurds.

*   *   *

The investigations referenced in the foregoing were carried out according to accepted professional archaeological and anthropological standards, and the statements in the above report are true and correct to the best of our knowledge and belief.

Respectfully submitted,

James Briscoe
Forensic Team Archaeologist

Clyde Collins Snow
Forensic Team Scientific Leader

APPENDIX 2

Summary of Anthropological Report

by

Clyde Collins Snow,
Forensic Team Scientific Leader

Introduction

The following discussion summarizes exhumations undertaken by the forensic team in Koreme, Birjinni, and Jeznikam-Beharke cemetery. The full scientific and forensic report on each exhumed skeleton may be obtained from MEW/PHR and will be submitted as evidence to any judicial tribunal hearing charges based on the foregoing report, "The Destruction of Koreme During the Anfal Campaign," the contents of which are incorporated by reference into this discussion.

Koreme

The forensic team exhumed 27 skeletons from two graves at Koreme. All 27 skeletons were male, ranging in age from early adolescent to approximately early 40s. All appeared to have suffered death by gunshot wounds.

In most of the 27 cases, detailed study of the fracture patterns in anatomical relation enabled the forensic team to determine the number of wounds suffered by each individual. Wherever possible, the forensic team also tried to establish the trajectory of the projectile.

As a first step in this analysis, fragmented bones were reconstructed with the aid of a hot glue gun. Reassembly of the thorax and vertebral column of each skeleton, also by gluing, was particularly useful in establishing trajectories of wounds involving these regions. Bullets or their fragments still embedded in the bones also provided certain clues. Bullet holes in the victims' garments, studied in relation to the observed osteological trauma, gave clearcut evidence of trajectories in many cases. These findings on a per skeleton basis are available in the full anthropological report.

In some cases, it was impossible -- due to the complexity of the fracture patterns -- to determine whether the trauma was to due to a single projectile or several. Thoracic wounds with widespread and multiple rib fractures are particularly apt to be ambiguous in this respect because it is so often difficult to determine whether the trauma was caused by more than one bullet or by fragments of a single bullet. In our analysis, such cases were classified as a single wound. Because of this, our final tabulation of the number of wounds observed may be an underestimate. Another source of possible error is due to the difficulty of diagnosing compound wounds. For example, from skeletal evidence alone, it may be impossible to determine whether a bullet passed through the forearm and continued to enter the chest. Therefore, some of the wounds we have included in our tabulation may represent compound wounds caused by a single bullet passing through two or more body segments. Finally, it must be recalled that a bullet may cause wounds without any discernible osteological trauma at all. It is not uncommon, for example, for projectiles to cause through-and-through abdominal wounds without striking bone.

In all, there was clearcut evidence of at least 84 separate wounds distributed among the 27 skeletons. Five, or 18.5%, of the series showed evidence of a single wound. In the remaining 22, the number of wounds ranged from two (seven individuals) to six (one individual) with an average of 3.1 wounds per individual.

The distribution of the identified wounds by body region shows that wounds of the upper trunk (thorax and shoulder) were most prevalent, making up 28.6% of the 84 observed. Fifteen wounds involved the pelvis (including the lower lumbar vertebra). Thus, in all, wounds of the trunk (thorax and pelvis) numbered 39 or nearly half (46.4%) of those observed. Wounds to the extremities made up 41.7% of those observed; there was no statistically significant difference in their distribution by region (15 were in the upper extremity and 20 in the lower) or side (15 left, 20 right). As pointed out above, many of these extremity wounds -- especially those of the upper arm and thigh -- were probably compound. Ten (11.9%) of the wounds were to the head.

Each of the identified wounds was studied to determine its trajectory. A given trajectory can be defined in terms of its directional components in relation to the principal anatomical axes. In two cases, trajectories were indeterminate, reducing the number of observations to 82 from the total of 84 wounds.

The distribution of the 82 observed wounds by direction shows the results of Chi-square tests on the data. Wounds from projectiles entering the front of the body and those entering from the back were nearly equal in number. The same is true for those entering from the right and the left. However, wounds with downward trajectories occurred over twice as frequently as those from projectiles passing upward and this difference is strongly significant (p < .001).

The anatomical distribution of wounds observed in the 27 victims suggests a random and indiscriminate firing pattern with the principal aiming points in the trunk. This is also supported by the anatomical distribution of the observed wounds. Of particular interest is the low frequency of head wounds, suggesting that the traditional coup de grace, in the form of a single gunshot wound to the head, was not systematically rendered in this case.

Trajectories are also revealing. For example, the statistically significant preponderance of downward-passing bullet paths indicates that the shooters fired from a position somewhat higher than the victims. although bullets entering from the front of the body and from the back caused about an equal number of wounds, in almost all cases the transverse was the predominant vectorial component. Stated more simply, most of the wounds entered the side of the body rather than directly from the front or the back. This finding indicates that the victims were unrestrained and, perhaps reacting to visual stimuli (raising of firearms to a firing position) and/or auditory (a command to commence firing) cues, had already begun involuntarily to turn or twist away from the executioners when first struck.

In summary, the ballistic and wound evidence is consistent with the accounts given by survivors and other witnesses.

Birjinni

Investigations were undertaken in Birjinni for the limited purpose of determining whether forensic data was consistent with villagers' accounts of chemical weapons attacks in August 1992 resulting in four deaths and an undetermined number of injuries. The purpose of exhumations was to find out whether any traces of chemical agents remained on the clothing of victims after four years of burial, in the case of victims who had been buried unwashed and in their original clothing relatively soon after death from chemical agents. Birjinni was thus selected as the investigation site on account of survivor reports that two victims, an old man and a boy, had fallen victim to chemical agents and buried shortly thereafter in their original clothing.

The forensic team exhumed skeletons from two adjacent graves at Koreme, following standard procedures. The first skeleton was determined to be that of an old man, of approximately sixty years. Surviving family members identified the remains as those of the grandfather, on the basis of artifacts and clothing. The second skeleton was that of a young boy, of approximately five years. Family members identified the remains as those of the son, on the basis of clothing. Examination of the skeleton revealed no signs of trauma or perimortem violence, or any other indication inconsistent with accounts of the chemical weapons attack given by surviving villagers. Laboratory analysis has thus far been unable to detect any signs of chemical agents in clothing, soil, or bone samples.

Jeznikam

The forensic team undertook three exhumations in the detainee sector of Jeznikam cemetery for the purpose of determining whether forensic evidence would reveal any indications inconsistent with accounts of detention, and resulting privation and death, described by surviving detainees. The forensic team was accompanied in its Jeznikam investigations by a Koreme villager who said he had buried his mother and infant sister, Farwan Tawa Mostafa, in the detainee sector of the cemetery.

The forensic team exhumed at the site where the Koreme villager indicated he had buried Farwan. The team encountered the skeleton of a female infant, interred in a dress identified by the Koreme villager as the one in which he had buried his sister.

The mandibular central incisors of the skeleton were almost completely erupted and the maxillary centrals unerupted, suggesting an age at death of around seven (plus or minus four) months. However, using diaphysial length of the long bones as an aging criteria, Farwan would have been classified as no more than 1-3 months old. This marked discrepancy between dental and skeletal age is diagnostic of severe nutritional and/or disease stress since, in such cases, dental maturation tends to remain in step with chronological age while skeletal growth is severely retarded. The bones displayed no signs of perimortem violence.

100

Accordingly, the forensic team finds that Farwan Tawa Mostafa was a female infant likely suffering from severe malnutrition or disease. The forensic team found no evidence inconsistent with accounts given by detainee survivors.

*   *   *

The investigations summarized above were carried out in accordance with accepted anthropological standards. A complete report, including data for each exhumed skeleton, is available from MEW and PHR. The statements and conclusions above are true and correct to the best of my knowledge and belief.

Respectfully submitted,

Clyde Collins Snow,
Forensic Team Scientific Leader

APPENDIX 3

Firearms Identification
of the Koreme Execution Site

by

Douglas D. Scott, Ph.D.
Lincoln, Nebraska

The cartridge cases, totaling 124, from the Koreme execution site were analyzed to determine the minimum number of shooters. Sixty-three cases were collected from the site surface and their location was piece-plotted. The piece-plotting proved valuable in ascertaining movement of individual guns during the execution. These cases were identified by a number (1 to 63) written on the case body in indelible ink.

Seventeen additional cases were recovered during the excavation of Grave B-S. They were separately bagged when received. A letter (A through Q) was arbitrarily assigned by the author. The letter was written on the case body with a fine point Sharpie. A final group of cases totaled 44. These were recovered in pile near an olive oak tree about 20 meters north of the piece-plotted cartridge cases. For convenience these cases were arbitrarily numbered (100 through 143) with a Sharpie.

Methods of Analysis

The comparative study of ammunition components is known as firearms identification analysis. Firearms, in their discharge, leave behind distinctive metallic fingerprints or signatures on the ammunition components. These signatures, called class characteristics, allow the determination of the type of firearm (i.e. model or brand) in which a given cartridge case or bullet was fired. This then allows determination of the number of different types of guns used in a given situation.

Further, they allow the identification of individual weapons by comparing the unique qualities of firearm signatures, individual characteristics. This capability is very important because coupled with the precise artifact locations, identical signatures can be used to identify specific firing areas. With this information, patterns of movement can be established and sequences of activity can be more precisely interpreted.

The means to this end is reasonably simple in concept. When a cartridge weapon is fired the firing pin strikes the primer contained in the cartridge, leaving a distinctive imprint on the case. The primer ignites the powder, thus forcing the bullet down the barrel. The rifling in the barrel imprints the lands and grooves on the bullet in mirror image. The extractor also imprints the spent case as it is removed, extracted, from the gun's chamber. These imprints are called individual characteristics.

Police agencies have long used the investigative technique of firearms identification as an aid in solving crimes. Two methods commonly used by police departments include comparisons of bullets and cartridge cases (Harris 1980; Hatcher, Jury, and Weller 1977) to identify weapon types from which they were fired. Police are routinely successful in matching bullets and/or cartridge case individual characteristics to the crime weapon simply by demonstrating that the firing pin, extractor marks, or the land and groove marks could only have been made by a certain weapon. In the event that weapons used in a crime are not recovered, police can say with certainty, on the basis of the individual characteristics, from recovered bullets and cases, that specific types and numbers of weapons were used.

The comparison microscope is critical to the analysis of ammunition. Simply, the microscope is constructed so that two separate microscope tubes are joined by a bridge with prisms mounted over the tubes. Two separate images are transmitted to the center of the bridge, where another set of prisms transmit the images to central eyepieces. The eyepieces are divided so that each image appears on one-half of the eyepieces. Movable stages allow the objects under scrutiny to be manipulated so that they can be directly compared for class and individual characteristics.

The microscope used in this analysis was a Bausch and Lomb comparison microscope. The objectives range from 10 to 50 power. Each cartridge case was examined to determine its class characteristics. The cases were all fired in a 7.62-caliber firearm. The cases appear to have been fired in a semi-automatic or full automatic gun like the AK-47. All cases were fired in similar type firearms.

Following class characteristics determination the cases were compared to one another to determine individual characteristics. When possible matches were identified these cases were set aside until the sequence of initial identification was completed. Then each group was re-analyzed. Once a case group, arbitrarily numbered one through seven, was verified, two to three cases from each group were then compared to the other groups to further cross-check identification validity.

Results of Analysis

The firearms identification analysis indicate there were at least seven individual firearms used in the execution. The firearms were all semi-automatic or full automatic 7.62 x 39 mm caliber firearms. Multiple matches were made with all cases. The seventeen cases found in the grave and the 44 found near the olive tree matched to the piece-plotted cases. The firearms evidence strongly suggests only a single event involving the firing of over 100 rounds of 7.62mm caliber ammunition occurred at this site. Those involved in the shooting are minimally identified as seven individuals.

Table 1 identifies the case groupings that match. The matching groups were arbitrarily numbered one through seven. Among the cases are five unfired rounds (1, 15, 17, 62, and 63) found intermixed with the fired rounds. A single cartridge (number 16) was a misfire. Individual number 4 fired at least 15 rounds. Some time during the shooting he had a round misfire that required it be cleared from the chamber by manually working the firing bolt. The condition of his gun's firing pin, as seen in the imprint on the primer, strongly suggests this gun was very dirty and possibly in poor condition.

The AK-47 and similar model firearms have a detachable magazine that contains 30 rounds. Assuming each shooter had loaded a 30 round magazine in his weapon prior to the execution it appears that individuals 1, 2, 3, 4, 5, and 7 fired at least one partial magazine each. Recovered cases indicated each minimally fired between 12 and 17 rounds, which is approximately one-half of a full magazine. Individual number 6 fired at least 37 rounds. This individual had to reload at least once during the execution.

The distribution of the cases, as piece-plotted shows two distinct clusters of cases. One group of six or seven cases lies in a western cluster. The second and largest group is 16 meters to the east. A possible third cluster lies in a rough line to the north of the western group. There is a gap of about 16 meters between the eastern and western clusters where only a single case, number 11 was found.

105

When the case matches are plotted it becomes clear that the separation of cases is more apparent than real. Five individuals (numbers 3, 4, 5, 6, and 7) fired in the eastern and western clusters. The plotted matches in the western cluster suggest the individuals were aligned in a somewhat linear arrangement in this area. The eastern group demonstrates a much more bunched grouping.

I speculate that the firing squad may have been a linear arrangement on the west and as the firing began the men moved to the east in a random manner. The absence of cases between the west and east may be artificial in that the cases found in the grave and piled near the tree may imply someone picked the central area nearly clean.

The case distribution and matches make it clear that individuals number 2, 4, 6, and 7 moved to the north from the western cluster and fired one or more rounds each as they neared the victim line. Individual number 6 fired at least 12 rounds as he moved toward the victim line. At least two rounds were fired within ten meters or less of the victim line by individual number 6.

In conclusion the cartridge case firearms identification analysis from the Koreme execution site indicate at least seven individuals were responsible for the shooting. The collection and piling of a large quantity of cases has undoubtedly disrupted the overall pattern so all conclusions presented are subject to this bias. Six of the seven individuals fired at least one partial 30 round magazine during the execution. One individual fired one whole and at least one partial magazine during the shooting. Individual number 6, who fired the most rounds, also moved the closest to the victim line as determined from the piece-plotted cases.

Table 1
Case Matches Among the Koreme Site Cartridges

Group	Matching Cases by Number
1.	2, 4, 6, 8, 9, 20, 23, 49, 106, 109, 111, 137 (total 12)
2.	3, 7, 24, 28, 31, 36, 41, 54, 113, 128, 140, 141 (total 12)
3.	5, 25, 29, 32, 34, 37, 40, 47, 48, 112, 120, G, J, (total 13)
4.	10, 12, 14, 16 (misfire), 59, 102, 110, 121, 126, 127, D, F, H, L, N, (total 15)
5.	13, 18, 19, 21, 22, 104, 114, 138, A, B, C, I, K, M, O, P, Q (total 17)
6.	11, 26, 44, 45, 46, 50, 51, 52, 53, 56, 57, 58, 60, 61, 100, 101, 103, 105, 107, 108, 115, 116, 117, 118, 119, 122, 123, 124, 125, 129, 130, 131, 132, 134, 136, 139, 142 (total 37)
7.	27, 30, 33, 35, 38, 39, 42, 43, 55, 133, 135, 143, E (total 13)

References Cited

Harris, C.E.
1980 Sherlock Holmes Would Be Impressed. *American Rifleman* 128(5):36-39, 82.

Hatcher, Julian, Frank J. Jury, and Jac Weller
1977 *Firearms Investigation, Identification and Evidence.* Harrisburg, Pa.: Stackpole Books

Convention on the Prevention and Punishment of the Crime of Genocide

Approved and proposed for signature and ratification or accession by General Assembly resolution 260 A(III) of 9 December 1948

ENTRY INTO FORCE: 12 January 1951, in accordance with article XIII

The Contracting Parties,

Having considered the declaration made by the General Assembly of the United Nations in its resolution 96 (I) dated 11 December 1946 that genocide is a crime under international law, contrary to the spirit and aims of the United Nations and condemned by the civilized world,

Recognizing that at all periods of history genocide has inflicted great losses on humanity, and

Being convinced that, in order to liberate mankind from such an odious scourge, international co-operation is required,

Hereby agree as hereinafter provided:

Article I

The Contracting Parties confirm that genocide, whether committed in time of peace or in time of war, is a crime under international law which they undertake to prevent and to punish.

Article II

In the present Convention, genocide means any of the following acts committed with intent to destroy, in whole or in part, a national, ethnical, racial or religious group, as such:

(a) Killing members of the group;

(b) Causing serious bodily or mental harm to members of the group;

(c) Deliberately inflicting on the group conditions of life calculated to bring about its physical destruction in whole or in part;

(d) Imposing measures intended to prevent births within the group;

(e) Forcibly transferring children of the group to another group.

Article III

The following acts shall be punishable:

(a) Genocide;

(b) Conspiracy to commit genocide;

(c) Direct and public incitement to commit genocide;

(d) Attempt to commit genocide;

(e) Complicity in genocide.

Article IV

Persons committing genocide or any of the other acts enumerated in article III shall be punished, whether they are constitutionally responsible rulers, public officials or private individuals.

Article V

The Contracting Parties undertake to enact, in accordance with their respective Constitutions, the necessary legislation to give effect to the provisions of the present Convention, and, in particular, to provide effective penalties for persons guilty of genocide or any of the other acts enumerated in article III.

Article VI

Persons charged with genocide or any of the other acts enumerated in article III shall be tried by a competent tribunal of the State in the territory of which the act was committed, or by such international penal tribunal as may have jurisdiction with respect to those Contracting Parties which shall have accepted its jurisdiction.

Article VII

Genocide and the other acts enumerated in article III shall not be considered as political crimes for the purpose of extradition.

The Contracting Parties pledge themselves in such cases to grant extradition in accordance with their laws and treaties in force.

Article VIII

Any Contracting Party may call upon the competent organs of the United Nations to take such action under the Charter of the United Nations as they consider appropriate for the prevention and suppression of acts of genocide or any of the other acts enumerated in article III.

Article IX

Disputes between the Contracting Parties relating to the interpretation, application or fulfilment of the present Convention, including those relating to the responsibility of a State for genocide or for any of the other acts enumerated in article III, shall be submitted to the International Court of Justice at the request of any of the parties to the dispute.

Article X

The present Convention, of which the Chinese, English, French, Russian and Spanish texts are equally authentic, shall bear the date of 9 December 1948.

Article XI

The present Convention shall be open until 31 December 1949 for signature on behalf of any Member of the United Nations and of any non-member State to which an invitation to sign has been addressed by the General Assembly.

The present Convention shall be ratified, and the instruments of ratification shall be deposited with the Secretary-General of the United Nations.

After 1 January 1950, the present Convention may be acceded to on behalf of any Member of the United Nations and of any non-member State which has received an invitation as aforesaid.

Instruments of accession shall be deposited with the Secretary-General of the United Nations.

Article XII

Any Contracting Party may at any time, by notification addressed to the Secretary-General of the United Nations, extend the application of the present Convention to all or any of the territories for the conduct of whose foreign relations that Contracting Party is responsible.

Article XIII

On the day when the first twenty instruments of ratification or accession have been deposited, the Secretary-General shall draw up a *proces-verbal* and transmit a copy thereof to each Member of the United Nations and to each of the non-member States contemplated in article XI.

The present Convention shall come into force on the ninetieth day following the date of deposit of the twentieth instrument of ratification or accession.

Any ratification or accession effected, subsequent to the latter date shall become effective on the ninetieth day following the deposit of the instrument of ratification or accession.

Article XIV

The present Convention shall remain in effect for a period of ten years as from the date of its coming into force.

It shall thereafter remain in force for successive periods of five years for such Contracting Parties as have not denounced it at least six months before the expiration of the current period.

Denunciation shall be effected by a written notification addressed to the Secretary-General of the United Nations.

Article XV

If, as a result of denunciations, the number of Parties to the present Convention should become less than sixteen, the Convention shall cease to be in force as from the date on which the last of these denunciations shall become effective.

Article XVI

A request for the revision of the present Convention may be made at any time by any Contracting Party by means of a notification in writing addressed to the Secretary-General.

The General Assembly shall decide upon the steps, if any, to be taken in respect of such request.

Article XVII

The Secretary-General of the United Nations shall notify all Members of the United Nations and the non-member States contemplated in article XI of the following:

(a) Signatures, ratifications and accessions received in accordance with article XI;

(b) Notifications received in accordance with article XII;

(c) The date upon which the present Convention comes into force in accordance with article XIII;

(d) Denunciations received in accordance with article XIV;

(e) The abrogation of the Convention in accordance with article XV;

(f) Notifications received in accordance with article XVI.

Article XVIII

The original of the present Convention shall be deposited in the archives of the United Nations.

A certified copy of the Convention shall be transmitted to each Member of the United Nations and to each of the non-member States contemplated in article XI.

Article XIX

The present Convention shall be registered by the Secretary-General of the United Nations on the date of its coming into force.

APPENDIX 5

Memorandum:

The Elements of Crimes Against Humanity Applied to the Destruction of Koreme

Human Rights Watch ("HRW") understands the legal elements of crimes against humanity, applied to events described in the foregoing report "The Destruction of Koreme During the Anfal Campaign, "(The Destruction of Koreme") as follows.

Elements of Crimes Against Humanity

Crimes against humanity are defined as[1]:

---

[1] This definition is adapted from article 6(c) of the Charter of the International Military Tribunal (the "Nuremberg Tribunal"), art. 6(c), as amended by the Berlin Protocol, 59 Stat. 1546, 1547 (1945), E.A.S. No. 472, 82 U.N.T.S. 284 (the "Nuremberg Charter"), which reads as follows:

> "[Crimes against humanity are] murder, extermination, enslavement, deportation, and other inhumane acts committed against any civilian population, before or during the war, or persecutions on political, racial, or religious grounds in execution of or in connection with any crime within the jurisdiction of the Tribunal, whether or not in violation of the domestic law of the country where perpetrated."

The definition in the text above takes into account limiting interpretations of certain terms by the Nuremberg Tribunal, as well as other Allied war crimes tribunals interpreting similar language following the end of World War II, and so is narrower than the article 6(c) definition. See generally Orentlicher, "Settling Accounts: The Duty to Prosecute Human Rights Violations of Prior Regime," 100 *Yale L.J.* 2537, 2585 (1991) ("Orentlicher"); Bassiouni, "International Law and the Holocaust," 9 *Cal. West. Int'l. L.J.* 201 (1979); Schwelb, "Crimes Against Humanity," 23 *Brit. Y.B. Int'l. L.* 178 (1946); and Clark, "Crimes Against Humanity," *The Nuremberg Trial and International Law*, ed. Ginsburgs and Kudriartser (1990) ("Clark"). For general accounts of crimes against humanity in the historical context of the Nuremberg trials, see generally Taylor, *The Anatomy of the Nuremberg Trials*, Alfred A. Knopf, 1992; Tusa and Tusa, *The Nuremberg Trial*, Atheneum, 1984; Smith, *The Road to Nuremberg*, Basic Books, 1981; and Conot,

(i) Such crimes as murder, extermination, enslavement, and deportation, and other similarly inhumane acts; or

(ii) persecutions on political, racial, or religious grounds, but which are of a nature not less serious than the foregoing crimes described in (i);

(iii) committed against any civilian population whether in conformity with or in violation of domestic law governing such civilians; and

(iv) committed on a mass scale.[2]

Justice at Nuremberg, Harper & Row, 1983.

[2] In the opinion of HRW, the definition of crimes against humanity does not include a necessary connection to war, meaning that it is possible for crimes against humanity to occur in times of peace. It is the view of HRW that the Nuremberg Tribunal's refusal to adjudicate alleged crimes against German nationals by the German government prior to the outbreak of war in 1939 was by reason of the Nuremberg Tribunal's understanding of the limits of its jurisdiction under the Nuremberg Charter, and not because it understood crimes against humanity, as an international crime, to exist by definition solely in time of war. A tribunal otherwise competent to hear crimes against humanity is therefore not disabled solely on the ground that the acts alleged as crimes against humanity did not occur in connection with war. The so-called "war-nexus" is thus not included in the definition of crimes against humanity given in the text above.

In support of the view that the "war-nexus" is either no longer legally relevant or was, at the time of the Nuremberg Tribunal, jurisdictional only and not definitional, see Orentlicher at 2590; Clark at 195-6; and the Fourth Report on the Draft Code of Offences Against the Peace and Security of Mankind by Mr. Doudou Thiam, 38 U.N. GAOR C.4 at 56, U.N. Doc. A/CN.4/398 (1986) D. Thiam "the separation of crimes against humanity from war crimes has now become absolute. Today, crimes against humanity can be committed not only within the context of an armed conflict, but also independently of any such conflict").

HRW does not here address the question of whether crimes against humanity must be committed by individuals acting in some degree as agents of a state. The Judgment of the Nuremberg Tribunal and related precedents are absolutely clear that individuals may incur liability for crimes against humanity, and that an individual is not shielded from liability for crimes against humanity by acting under color of the state. It is less clear, however, whether an individual could plead immunity from the charge of crimes against humanity on the ground

Crimes Against Humanity and the Destruction of Koreme

It is evident that events described in "The Destruction of Koreme" qualify as crimes within the meaning of elements (i)-(iii) above: the inhabitants of Koreme and Birjinni were murdered, the case of the men of Koreme by firing squad at their own village; they were exterminated, including extermination with chemical weapons; and they were deported to the camps of Jeznikam and Beharke, on ethnic grounds. Large numbers of men and boys from Koreme were forcibly disappeared while in the custody of the Iraqi security agents and have never reappeared, which HRW finds to be murder by any other name. Thus element (i) is met, and because, moreover, they suffered them in the course of persecutions on racial grounds -- for being Kurds -- the persecution element (ii) is also met.[3]

Element (iii) of the definition of crimes against humanity establishes that it is legally irrelevant, in defining the crime, that the victims were Iraqi civilians and that their crimes were committed under color of Iraqi domestic law.

The "Mass Scale" Requirement

Accordingly, the only element left to be met for events described in "The Destruction of Koreme" to qualify as crimes against humanity is element (iv), that they have been committed on a mass scale. HRW takes no position on the question of how few crimes committed in the pursuit of elements (i)-(iii) are required to constitute a "mass scale" within the definition of crimes against humanity. HRW has no reason to do so because the crimes undertaken by the Anfal campaign were so vast that

---

of having no relationship, direct or indirect, formal or informal, with a state. HRW need not settle whether it considers this a necessary element because in the case of Iraqi government crimes in Koreme, as at Nuremberg, there is no question but that all the alleged authors of these crimes acted directly as agents of the state.

[3] Note, however, that the element of persecution is an alternative ground for finding crimes against humanity, and not an additional requirement to element (i), so long as the persecutions comprise crimes not less serious than murder, extermination, enslavement, and deportation provided in element (i).

they render any determination of a minimal level superfluous.

Although "The Destruction of Koreme" makes only passing reference to the full extent of the Anfal campaign, HRW has in its files hundreds of interviews conducted by its investigators demonstrating beyond any reasonable doubt the destruction of thousands of Kurdish villages, and the murder, forcible disappearance, extermination by chemical weapons, extermination by chemical weapons, or forcible resettlement of hundreds of thousands of Kurds. These interviews will be summarized in future Middle East Watch reports, but HRW is wholly satisfied, as a matter of law, that the "mass scale" requirement of crimes against humanity has been met.

It should be noted that "The Destruction of Koreme" does not take a position on whether genocide occurred in Iraqi Kurdistan, although the report observes that MEW's investigations are steadily leading to that conclusion. The reason for this circumspection with respect to genocide is that genocide requires a specific intent to destroy a protected group "in whole or in part...as such."[4] Proving such intent requires more than the limited findings required to prove crimes against humanity.

HRW believes the evidence is clear that such crimes as murder, disappearance, and deportation took place in the course of ethnic persecution against the Kurds of Iraq on a mass scale sufficient to meet the threshold of crimes against humanity. The other elements of crimes against humanity being met, HRW concludes that the crimes described in "The Destruction of Koreme" constitute crimes against humanity within the meaning of customary international law.[5]

---

[4] See the Convention on the Punishment and Prevention of the Crime of Genocide, entered into force January 12, 1951, at Article II.

[5] HRW reserves on the question of what entity, if any, has legal jurisdiction to try the alleged authors of crimes against humanity.